T0313029

ROUTLEDGE LIBRARY EDITIONS: INDUSTRIAL RELATIONS

Volume 31

THE POLICY-MAKING PROCESS

THE POLICY-MAKING PROCESS

J.J. RICHARDSON

Routledge
Taylor & Francis Group

LONDON AND NEW YORK

First published in 1969 by Routledge & Kegan Paul Ltd

This edition first published in 2025
by Routledge
4 Park Square, Milton Park, Abingdon, Oxon OX14 4RN

and by Routledge
605 Third Avenue, New York, NY 10158

Routledge is an imprint of the Taylor & Francis Group, an informa business

© 1969 J.J. Richardson

All rights reserved. No part of this book may be reprinted or reproduced or utilised in any form or by any electronic, mechanical, or other means, now known or hereafter invented, including photocopying and recording, or in any information storage or retrieval system, without permission in writing from the publishers.

Trademark notice: Product or corporate names may be trademarks or registered trademarks, and are used only for identification and explanation without intent to infringe.

British Library Cataloguing in Publication Data
A catalogue record for this book is available from the British Library

ISBN: 978-1-032-81770-5 (Set)
ISBN: 978-1-032-81237-3 (Volume 31) (hbk)
ISBN: 978-1-032-81238-0 (Volume 31) (pbk)
ISBN: 978-1-003-49878-0 (Volume 31) (ebk)

DOI: 10.4324/9781003498780

Publisher's Note
The publisher has gone to great lengths to ensure the quality of this reprint but points out that some imperfections in the original copies may be apparent.

Disclaimer
The publisher has made every effort to trace copyright holders and would welcome correspondence from those they have been unable to trace.

The Policy-making Process

by J. J. Richardson

Lecturer in Politics
University of Keele

LONDON
ROUTLEDGE & KEGAN PAUL
NEW YORK: HUMANITIES PRESS

First published 1969
by Routledge & Kegan Paul Ltd
Broadway House, 68-74 Carter Lane
London, E.C.4
Printed in Great Britain
by Northumberland Press Limited
Gateshead
© *J. J. Richardson 1969*
No part of this book may be reproduced
in any form without permission from
the publisher, except for the quotation
of brief passages in criticism

SBN 7100 6523 x

General editor's introduction

This series of monographs is designed primarily to meet the needs of students of government, politics, or political science in Universities and other institutions providing courses leading to degrees. Each volume aims to provide a brief general introduction indicating the significance of its topic e.g. executives, parties, pressure groups, etc., and then a longer 'case study' relevant to the general topic. First year students will thus be introduced to the kind of detailed work on which all generalizations must be based, while more mature students will have an opportunity to become acquainted with recent original research in a variety of fields. The series will eventually provide a comprehensive coverage of most aspects of political science in a more interesting and fundamental manner than in the large volume which often fails to compensate by breadth what it inevitably lacks in depth.

This study of 'The Making of the Restrictive Trade Practices Act 1956' is an addition to the still rather limited number of case studies of the British governmental process. It examines the various interests both private and public that were concerned with restrictive trade practices. There

is a full discussion of the report of the Monopolies Commission and of the public discussion which followed. In
view of the current interest in the legislative process and of
the influences which lead to particular pieces of legislation,
the section dealing with the passage of the Bill through Parliament is particularly revealing. Finally there are some useful references to the constraints within which public policy
has to be formed and to the interrelationship between
interest groups and the Government which purports to represent the public interest. This volume should be of the
utmost interest, not merely to students but to all those who
are concerned with the decision-making processes in this
country.

H.V.W.

Contents

Acknowledgements

I should like the thank the Editor of *Parliamentary Affairs* for permission to use some of the material contained in my article for that Journal in Autumn 1967. Thanks are also due to H.M.S.O. for the table on the Monopolies Commission Report on Collective Discrimination, Cmd. 9504, which is reproduced in Chapter 4.

1
Introduction

The Restrictive Trade Practices Act of 1956 was an attempt by the Conservative government to increase the degree of competition within certain sections of British industry. It involved the Conservative party in an attack on organized industrial groups, which are commonly regarded as its natural allies. This study therefore attempts to throw some light on their interrelationships. The Act reflects a long-standing belief in Britain that the degree of competition and the efficient use of resources are closely related, and that restrictions on competition are against the welfare of the country. The Government's solution to the problem of restrictionism was to create the Restrictive Practices Court, an unusual innovation in the field of economic policy in that problems which were a confused mixture of economic, social, and political judgement, were handed over to a judicial court, and hence were removed from the influence and control of Parliament and Government.

The policy-making process, leading up to the passage of the Act, is an interesting example of the interaction between politics and economics in a system of interest-group consultation. The legislation attacked the long-established practices of certain industrial trade associations. These associations had a long history of extremely close co-operation with various government departments, so much so in fact that in many ways the government has become dependent upon this co-operation in the day-to-day administration of its policy. Conversely, the associations themselves in turn become dependent upon the government as government support for industry increases. In this way a system of mutual inter-dependence between government and interest groups has developed. One aim of this study is to analyse the way in which agreement is reached when the government and interest groups occupying key positions in the economy come into conflict.

The wider purpose of this study is however to look at a much broader field than just the activity of interest groups and the part they play in the policy process, because, even though very important, group influence is only one of the factors which influence policy making.

As will be seen an attempt has been made to examine what has often been called the cultural context within which the process was enacted. D. Easton (*World Politics* 1956/7) suggests that no part of the larger political canvas stands alone, but is related to every other part. Because of this, it is impossible to analyse any particular example of the policy-making process at a given point in time, without some reference to previous decisions and attitudes. These certainly influenced the working of the process in 1956. In this case the attitude of the public and the press towards certain trade association activities must also be considered as a factor surrounding the whole process of decision-making. In this context it is interesting to note the complex relationship between the press and opinion formation, and the consequent role that the press can play in influencing the behaviour of politicians.

It is also important to try to assess the role of the permanent bureaucracy in the policy process—in this case the Board of Trade. This is of course extremely difficult to do. This example of the policy process does however raise some interesting problems concerning role conflict which may arise within a government department which finds itself responsible for a policy which is being opposed by its clients. Role conflict can also arise within Parliament when M.P.s find themselves faced with conflicting loyalties (Epstein, L. D., 1964, 6). Many Conservative M.P.s were members of trade associations likely to be affected by the proposed legislation. As industrialists, they sincerely believed that the practices under attack were in the interests of the country as a whole, quite apart from being also in the interests of the members of a given association. But as Conservatives, they were called upon to support the government in its policy.

It is intended in this study to try to take account of all the factors outlined above, so that an overall view of an example of policy making can emerge. There are, of course inherent difficulties in the case study approach. Firstly, it is impossible to make broad generalizations from one case study, since at another point in time various factors will almost certainly have changed. An example of this is public opinion, which often plays no part in policy making. Secondly, it is never possible to construct a complete account of the process, as a great deal of information is not available to research workers—for example, Cabinet records have not yet been published. Thirdly, many details of the consultative process between interest groups and the government have now disappeared from record or from memory. The memory factor is a particularly important limitation on this type of research, as much of the consultative process is not in the form of the written word, but takes place on an informal person-to-person basis, and the major part of this crucial aspect of the political process goes unrecorded. However, despite these limitations, it is hoped that students of British government will be given some insight into the complexity and workings of the policy process in Britain.

2
The problem and its historical development

The problem of restrictive practices is basically an
economic rather than a social or political problem, but
as with many other economic problems, political solutions
have to be formulated. Competition has long been
favoured and monopoly condemned by the majority of
economists. However, the model of perfect competition
does not describe the real world of the twentieth century
and most western countries have developed a system of
legislation designed to maintain competitive forces within
their economies (although it should be noted that not all
modern economists are agreed on the merits of competition). In practice in certain industries, individual firms
have either established a monopoly or have managed to
dominate the market to a considerable degree. In a
similar way, private associations, initially with government approval had, by the 1950s, created a situation of
conflict between public and private aims. This conflict
arose partly because Britain's economic position had

changed over the years. A major criticism of British industry in the post-war situation was that it had become uncompetitive in world markets. The attitude of politicians and civil servants had also changed so that after the Second World War trade associations found themselves faced with a rather more hostile attitude on the part of policy makers.

Private firms had contrived together, as trade associations, to institute some form of control over market forces in their respective industries. Such controls, loosely termed restrictive practices, were essentially an attempt by producers to attain some degree of control over market forces which individually they could not exert. Particularly significant in the 1950s was the group of practices known as collective discrimination. These were restrictions and sanctions applied collectively against firms that did not comply with trade associations rules. The rules covered various trading methods and for example often controlled both price and level of output. Before sanctions were applied by an association, offending firms or traders were tried before the trade association court. If a trader were found guilty he could be fined or placed on a stop list which meant that the supplies of goods to him would be cut off. It was this particular aspect of collective discrimination which was in large part responsible for making restrictive practices a live political issue.

THE GROWTH OF COMBINATIONS AND ASSOCIATIONS 1900-1948

The restrictive practices dealt with in the 1956 Bill had developed long before the 1950s. The trend towards restrictions can be traced back as far as the late nineteenth century (see Allen, G. C., in Chamberlin, 1954). They were sufficient in number in the 1880s for Joseph Chamberlain as President of the Board of Trade to instruct his officials to open direct personal contacts with them on all important matters of policy and day-to-day administration. J. Grove (1962) has suggested that this unprecedented step was the origin of the elaborate system of consultation with industry which is such an important feature of the British political system today. In a Fabian pamphlet of 1901, H. W. Macrosty, an early writer on the subject, warned against the dangers of increasing monopoly, despite its organizational advantages.

The movement towards combinations and concentration gained its real impetus during the First World War. Not only did the war help to create new trade associations, but it also brought them into much closer contact with the government and its departments. The process was often encouraged by the government, as the associations were found particularly useful in administering wartime controls. Such governmental encouragement of trade associations continued as a general trend up to and beyond the 1956 Act. Government policy towards such organizations has always been somewhat schizophrenic. From time to time governments have been worried about the degree of power the associations might wield within their industries while at the same time being anxious to preserve and encourage the associations as representative bodies.

However, by 1918 the government had begun to show some concern about the effect of trade organizations and combinations, and in that year the Ministry of Reconstruction appointed a Committee on Trusts to report on them. This Committee estimated that approximately 500 associations existed at the time, and reported that their power had been strengthened during the war. It also felt that there were inherent dangers in the trade association system and therefore recommended that the Board of Trade should be given wide powers of investigation. As a result of the Report the first of the Profiteering Acts was introduced in 1919. These Acts, though not monopoly legislation *per se*, certainly did set up machinery to deal with excessive control over market prices. They were designed to check the post-war tendency to increase retail prices of all kinds of commodities. Members of the public were allowed to lay charges before the Profiteering Committees. It is interesting to note that in many instances these charges were referred to the local Magistrates Court and in some cases the jurisdiction of the High Court was called upon. The Committees of Inquiry set up under the Act commented on the widespread nature of the arrangements for restricting competition. By 1920 the Board of Trade was in the process of drafting a Trading and Monopolies Bill although this was never introduced.

Post 1921: recession and depression

However, in 1921 the government allowed the Profiteering Acts to lapse. The problems of excessive demand in the economy had by then disappeared and the problem of the slump had become the overriding factor. The attitude to trusts and combines changed completely with the onset of depression and although a Trusts and Combines Bill was introduced by a private member as late as 1925, it did not become law. The attitude of hostility after the war changed to one of near complacency by 1929 when the Final Report of the Committee on Industry and Trade was published. The committee concluded that in the prevailing industrial situation, the case for legislation to restrain abuses which might result from combinations, was not an urgent one. Many restrictive agreements were introduced in the period as an answer to unemployment and depression. Depression made restrictionism respectable in the 1930s and governments, far from being concerned by this trend, wanted to encourage it. As J. W. Grove records (Grove, 1962, 46), the government sometimes enforced an amalgamation or helped create special restrictive institutions in lieu of trade associations. The abandonment of free trade of course helped industries to make schemes of control more effective.

One of the few dissenting voices amid the general trend of approval and encouragement in the 1920s and 1930s was that of the Liberal Industrial Inquiry Committee, which in 1928 published its report entitled 'Britain's Industrial Future'. Whilst the Report recognized the merits of monopoly, it proposed that where a company controlled fifty per cent or more of the market, it should be registered as a public corporation which would at intervals be subject to inspection by the Board of Trade. Similarly it was proposed that trade associations should conduct their operations under the watchful eye of the Board of Trade, which would be given power to publish any information of public interest or importance. However, even the Liberals were not in favour of a full-blooded attack on restrictionism. Their report considered that in certain cases it might be in the legitimate interests of a trade or industry for a small minority to be made to conform to the rules which the majority had decided to impose upon themselves. It therefore proposed that if in an association, seventy-five per cent of those affected

9

were in favour of a rule or instruction then, subject to the approval of the Board of Trade, the association should have statutory powers to enforce the rule throughout the industry.

Restrictionism and the courts

Throughout this period when restrictionism was being encouraged as an answer to unemployment, the common law doctrines of restraint of trade and conspiracy remained in force. Even as early as 1625, under the Statute of Monopolies, all monopolies, licences and letters patent for the sole buying, selling and making of anything in Britain had been void. However, from the beginning of the twentieth century, the courts had been increasingly inclined to listen to arguments in support of restrictive agreements. In the eighteenth century Lord Mansfield had declared that persons possessing any articles of trade could sell them at any price they pleased, but that if they confederated not to sell them under certain prices then it was a conspiracy. The judgements of the late nineteenth and twentieth centuries were very different. So in 1892 Lord Morris ruled that he entertained no doubt that a body of traders whose object was to promote their own trade, could combine to acquire, and thereby injure, the trade of competitors (Mogul Steamship Co. v. McGregor Gow & Co. [1892] A.C. 25). The case in question involved an association of shipowners who had joined together to divide cargoes and freight and to keep the shipping trade amongst themselves. In order to do this they sent a number of ships to ports where non-association firms were plying for trade, and undercut them so as to drive them out of business. The action of the association was upheld by the courts, as the agreement was in the interests of the contracting parties and was designed to increase their own trade. In 1909 the courts in similar vein, upheld the practice of exclusive dealing.

Four years later in 1913 Lord Parker remarked that their Lordships were not aware of any case in which a restraint, though reasonable in the interests of the parties, had been held to be unenforceable because it involved some injury to the public. Consequently he ruled that the right of the individual to carry out his trade or business in the way he considered best to further his own interests, involved the right to combine with others in a common course of action. The only proviso was that the common action should be undertaken solely with the interests of the combining parties in mind and not with a view to injuring others (Attorney-General of the Commonwealth of Australia v. Adelaide Steamship Co. Ltd. [1913] A.C. 78). Not only were the judges becoming more lenient, but some were quite prepared to make broad economic judgements as well. For example, Viscount Haldane expressed the view that an ill-regulated supply and unremunerative prices might be disadvantageous to the public. He thought that such a state of affairs, if it were not controlled, could drive manufacturers out of business, lower wages and cause unemployment (N.W. Salt Co. Ltd. v. Electrolytic Alkali Co. Ltd. [1914] A.C. 461). In 1937 the courts upheld that stop lists and fines could legitimately be used by trade associations. In Lord Thankerton's view it was quite legal and acceptable for an association to use stop lists in good faith for the furtherance or protection of its legitimate trade interests (Thorne v. Motor Trade Association [1937] A.C. 797).

The attitude of the courts in the period 1900-48 was

essentially that if a restrictive agreement were primarily designed to further the interests of the parties to the agreement; as opposed to being designed specifically to harm competitors, then it was legal. In fact the courts had by 1948, virtually abandoned their role of enforcing the common law restraints against monopoly and restrictive practices. This development is particularly relevant in that by 1955, when the government was ready to take action against restrictionism, the interest groups concerned put forward as one of their main demands, a suggestion that a judicial body should be responsible for the supervision of restrictive agreements.

DEVELOPMENTS 1948-54

The Second World War had (like the first) provided a further stimulus to trade association development. Trade associations were often responsible for the allocation of materials within an industry and were extremely important channels of communication between government and industry. In fact the government often actively encouraged the formation of more comprehensive trade associations. However, whereas during the war this process was viewed most favourably, when the problem of reconstruction began to be considered, the climate of opinion had changed, in government circles at least. Certain industries felt that the trade associations system should be extended, and they proposed that the government should authorize the establishment of a central authority with wide powers, for every industry. For example, the Sheffield cutlers proposed that a licensing scheme should be introduced to control new entrants. The government took a different attitude, and in May 1944 published its White Paper on

Full Employment Policy. It accepted as one of its primary aims, the maintenance of a high and stable level of employment and expressed the fear that an undue increase in prices might frustrate action taken to maintain full employment. It noted the growing trend over the years towards combines and agreements by which manufacturers sought to control prices and output, to divide markets and to fix conditions of sale. The government therefore announced that it would seek powers to inform itself of the extent and effect of restrictive agreements, and that it would take action to check practices which were advantageous to sectional producing interests, but worked to the detriment of the public at large.

The 1948 Act

The climate of opinion continued to change after 1944 and in March 1948 the government introduced the Monopolies and Restrictive Practices (Inquiry and Control) Bill, which received the Royal Assent in July of that year. The Act set up an independent Monopolies Commission consisting of ten members. The duty of the Commission was, at the suggestion of the Board of Trade, to investigate industries where at least one third of the supply, export or process of goods was controlled (a) by one person, firm or group of companies (b) by a restrictive agreement between firms or (c) by firms so conducting their business as to limit competition. Besides considering individual industries, the Commission could also be required, under Section 15 of the Act, to consider questions relating to the adoption of certain classes of restrictive practices by industry as a whole, and to report on their general effect on the public interest. It was this section that allowed the reference to be made which led to the 1955 Report. The Commission was charged with the duty of producing reports that the government would enforce, if it so decided. The Commission was appointed in January 1949 and received its first six references from the government a few months later.

Resale price maintenance

The report of the Committee on Resale Price Maintenance (the Lloyd Jacob Committee) was published during 1949. This Report recommended that no action should be taken which would deprive an individual producer of the power to enforce resale prices on his goods. The Committee felt however that collective enforcement of resale price maintenance had impeded development of economical trading methods and had prevented the reduction of costs and prices. It therefore recommended that the collective enforcement of resale price maintenance should be abolished. The findings of this report illustrate how much opinion had changed since the 1930s. In 1931 the Committee on Restraint of Trade (the Greene Committee) had concluded that there was no reason to think that a change in the law would benefit the public. After the publication of the Lloyd Jacob Committee Report, discussions took place between the Board of Trade and various trade associations. but the suggestions put forward by the associations failed to satisfy the government. As a result of this failure to reach agreements the government published a White Paper in June 1951, which indicated its intention of introducing legislation to ban both collective and individual enforcement of resale price maintenance (R.P.M.). This attitude was applauded by *The Economist* which thought that, if the government implemented the proposals set out in the White Paper, it would amount to a determined attack on one of the most obvious restrictive practices. But the government was defeated in the ensuing election so it was prevented from introducing the legislation. There was in fact some doubt as to whether the Labour party would have put its intentions into practice, because like the Conservatives, the party was divided on the issue.

THE POLITICAL PARTIES

As we have already seen, the Liberals had long campaigned for government intervention in this field. Both Labour and Conservatives were becoming increasingly aware of the problem throughout the 1950s, although neither had shown much enthusiasm in the early 1950s.

The Labour party

The Labour party proved to be particularly sensitive about the issue of R.P.M. The trade union side of the movement feared that the complete abolition of R.P.M. might cause unemployment in the distributive trades and production industries. The Union of Shop, Distributive and Allied Workers was particularly concerned on this point, and its representative defended the individual enforcement of R.P.M., when the issue was discussed at the 1952 Labour Conference. Similarly when the Monopolies Commission published a report in 1954 criticizing the calico printing industry, the President of the trade union in the industry declared that they had no intention of returning to the days of cut-throat competition. This was identical to the attitude of the employers in the industry. Nevertheless,

15

the party generally supported an attack on monopoly and restrictionism, and by 1955 Hugh Gaitskell had come out in favour of immediate action. His four point plan advocated (a) an increase in the size of the Monopolies Commission so that its work could be speeded up (b) greater powers of enforcement of Commission recommendations (c) total banning of what he called really vicious practices like stop lists and boycotts and (d) the compulsory publication of all trade association agreements. The attitude of the Labour party was to prove an important factor in the policy process, as will be explained in later chapters.

The Conservatives

The Conservative party has often campaigned as the party of free enterprise, and as such could be expected to support any policy designed to increase competition. To quote the Earl of Kilmuir 'as a free enterprise party we should be against private monopoly and restrictive practices' (Kilmuir, 1964, 154). The party had broadly supported the 1948 Bill, and had in 1951 severely criticized the slow working of the Commission under the Labour government, and indeed had in 1953 increased the size of the Commission to remedy this defect. Also a resolution submitted to the 1955 conference, called upon the government to tackle with vigour the evils of monopoly and restrictive practices on both sides of industry, without regard to pressure from interested parties.

But despite this generalized belief in competition, the party was divided on the issue of government action to curb restrictive practices. The party in Parliament contained many backbenchers who were themselves members of various restrictive trade associations, so that the step from generalized ideology to specific action, was likely to prove tortuous. Clearly those M.P.s connected with, or aligned with restrictive trade associations, were likely to oppose government action because they sincerely believed that such arrangements benefited both industry and the public at large. Equally clearly a number of Conservative backbenchers took the opposite view. For example, in 1954, ten backbenchers wrote a C.P.C. pamphlet called 'Change is Our Ally', which called for a vigorous attack on monopoly and restrictionism.

By 1955 the position of the two main parties was in many ways similar. They had both declared their eagerness to attack restrictionism and monopoly, yet had in practice shown hesitancy in implementing their general statements. Both parties tended to be split on the issue, though this was of far greater significance for the Conservatives. Both the Labour and Conservative parties were pledged to take further action. The form of action and the ensuing process are analysed in the following chapters.

3

The Monopolies Commission Report

The Monopolies Commission Report on Collective Discrimination (June 1955, Cmd. 9504) must be regarded as an extremely important influencing factor in the system. It not only formed the basis of the 1956 Act but also influenced much of the discussion prior to its passage. As will be shown in Chapter 4 the Report was published at a time when restrictive practices in trade and industry were already a controversial issue, and hence it served as an important stimulant to the claims for legislative action.

EVENTS LEADING TO THE INQUIRY

Since its inception, the Monopolies Commission had often been criticized for its slow rate of progress. This criticism was not confined to the Conservative's period of office, as some Labour backbenchers had been particularly scathing in their attack on their own government. Ted Leather (Conservative) had also attacked the Labour government for its lack of effective action and had argued that it was wrong to prohibit in one industry what was allowed in others. This sentiment was echoed by Sir Hugh Linstead (a Conservative M.P. who was connected with the drug industry) during a debate on the Dental Goods Order in 1951. In his view, if the practices condemned in the dental goods industry were to be declared illegal, 'they should be illegal either everywhere or nowhere'. The Association of Dental Goods Manufacturers had in fact sent a statement of its views to M.P.s, complaining that its practices, which had been condemned by the Commission, were going on unheeded in other industries. It is clear that there was a certain amount of injustice in the individual industries approach, as a situation existed, where industries carrying out such practices obtained a stay of execution simply because the Commission could not investigate them all at once.

There had also been increasing evidence of the need for a more general inquiry, as the five reports produced by the Commission prior to December 1952 had shown that certain practices were common to the five industries investigated. (Dental goods, electric lamps, insulated electric wires and cables, insulin, and cast iron rainwater goods.) They concluded that the practices concerned were generally against the public interest. The evidence reaching the Board of Trade by way of complaints also indicated that certain restrictive practices were fairly widespread in industry and trade. In fact Mr. Thorneycroft, the President of the Board of Trade, openly recognized that the accumulation of case studies 'might suggest that certain practices were prevalent' (Hansard, 23 July 1952) and that as a result certain 'authoritative general judgements ought to be formed and made known for the guidance of industry as a whole'. The first five reports had in fact done just this, i.e. suggested that

19

certain practices were widespread. However, as Mr. Thorneycroft suggested, it would have been difficult to draft legislation banning such practices on the evidence of just five reports. Hence the desirability of a general report to discover whether the conclusions reached in the first five reports were of general applicability.

Although the evidence compiled by late 1952 was not extensive, it was nonetheless sufficient to stimulate some pressure for further action. *The Economist*, for example, on the publication of the Report on Dental Goods, observed that there was no case for legislation against restrictionism in this field that was not also the case for legislation against similar practices in a large part of British industry (23 February 1951). Shortly after the return of a Conservative government in 1951, it called on the government to declare certain practices contrary to the public interest, with the added stipulation that associations or firms wishing to continue them should have to apply to the Monopolies Commission for exemption. Also it felt that there was increased public interest in the significance of trade associations. The individual Reports of the Commission were given wide press coverage as each appeared. Since the Commission condemned most of the practices as being against the public interest, it is likely that the government felt that public opinion would build up against it if the public thought that the government was dragging its feet on the issue. Just as the Labour party has at times suffered from its connections with the trade unions during unpopular strikes so the Conservative party has had to try to avoid being labelled the party of big business. Therefore, if only to appease parliamentary and press criticism, the government had to make some move in late 1952. What evidence there is in this case however, suggests that the Minister himself was keen to take some sort of action, so that it would be inaccurate to postulate a model of the policy process in which the government merely responds to events and pressures. Thus, on 17 December 1952, the Commission was asked to investigate the operation of various practices and arrangements concerned with exclusive dealing, collective boycotts, aggregated rebates and other discriminatory trade practices.

THE COMPOSITION OF THE COMMISSION

In 1955 the Commission consisted of sixteen members. But, under the terms of an amending Act of 1953, the Commission could be divided into groups, and the 1955 Report on Collective Discrimination was produced by only ten members of the Commission. The members of the group may be conveniently divided into six categories, according to their background and qualifications. This classification is not of course rigid as overlapping occurs in some instances. The most readily distinguishable categories were: (a) lawyers (b) economists (c) trade union representatives (d) businessmen (e) civil servants (f) previous committees and experience of Whitehall.

Lawyers. Lawyers were well represented in the group. The Chairman was Sir David Cairns who was called to the bar in 1926 and who became a K.C. in 1947. Sir Thomas Barnes was also a lawyer by profession, having been Treasury Solicitor 1934-53 and solicitor at the Board of Trade 1920-33. Mr. Brian Davidson, though primarily an industrialist had also received a legal training. Academic law was represented by Professor H. L. Goodhart, Pro-

21

fessor of Jurisprudence in the University of Oxford 1931-51.

Economists. Two academic economists were members of the group. Professor G. C. Allen had been Professor of Political Economy at the University of London since 1947 and was an authority on the structure of British industry. The other academic economist was Professor Sir Arnold Plant who was an authority on business administration.

Trade Unionists. Two members were connected with the trade union movement, Mr. A. J. Birch and Mr. C. N. Gallie. Mr. Birch was General Secretary of the Union of Shop, Distributive and Allied Workers (U.S.D.A.W.), a union long opposed to the abolition of the individual enforcement of R.P.M. As we have seen it had frequently disagreed with the Labour party on this issue. The official U.S.D.A.W. viewpoint in 1952 was that the abolition of R.P.M. would on balance have an adverse effect both on the public interest and on the interests of workers employed in the distributive trades. In a pamphlet produced in 1952 it had come out against any return to what it called nineteenth-century ideas on competition. Mr. Gallie had also been a trade union official, having been the General Secretary of the Railway Clerks Association and a member of the T.U.C. General Council.

Businessmen. In terms of direct industrial experience, the group was far more limited, Mr. Davidson being the only industrialist. He was a director of the Bristol Aeroplane Company. However, Mr. Gallie was also a part-time director of the nationalized concern, Cable and Wireless Ltd.

Civil Servants. Mr. C. H. P. Gifford had held posts in the Foreign Office. Sir Thomas Barnes had worked in the Treasury. Many of the other members of the group had been part-time civil servants during the war and in the immediate post-war period.

Previous Committees and Experience of Whitehall. Many members had gained experience of committee work, particularly on wartime and post-war committees concerned with industrial matters. Professor Allen had been a temporary Assistant Secretary at the Board of Trade 1941-44 and a member of the Central Price Regulation Committee 1944-53. Professor Goodhart had been Chairman of the Price Regulation Committee 1940-51. Sir Arnold Plant was a temporary civil servant during the period 1940-46 as adviser to the Ministerial Chairman of the Interdepartmental Materials Committee and was also a member of the Ministry of Works Committee on the Distribution of Building Materials 1946. Sir Richard Yeabsley had been accountant adviser to the Board of Trade and the Central Price Regulation Committee, and a member of the Lloyd Jacob Committee on R.P.M. (1949) which recommended the abolition of collective enforcement of R.P.M.

The above classification is not on the basis of interest-group representation. K. C. Wheare has suggested that where a committee is formulated to consider certain charges or allegations, then it is not advisable to appoint members directly connected with interest groups. He further argues, referring specifically to the Monopolies Commission, that it should be composed of impartial members, free from association with interested parties.

23

In fact the group investigating collective discrimination very nearly conformed to this ideal.

The people most concerned with the issue were industrialists, especially those who were members of trade associations operating the specific practices. Mr. Davidson was the only member coming directly from industry, and he cannot be described as an interest-group representative because the aircraft industry was not under investigation. This contrasts, for example, with the Beaver Committee on air pollution 1955 which included certain members of the National Society for Clean Air. This lack of any strong industrial representation had been criticized by industrialists in the past, and it may have reduced the Commission's credibility in industrial circles. However, in this case, a number of the members of the Commission had gained some experience of the working of industrial matters in their capacity as members of the various wartime committees concerned with industry. The two trade union members could be considered as interest-group representatives, although Mr. Gallie came from a nationalized industry which did not operate any of the practices being investigated. Mr. Birch on the other hand was likely to be more directly affected because of the attitude of his union.

Thus the group considering collective discrimination did not consist of representatives of those interest groups directly concerned with the issues (with the possible exception of Mr. Birch). One very notable absence was any obvious representative of the consumer interest though it would presumably have been very difficult to find a suitable person at that time. The problem of obtaining the consumer viewpoint arose particularly during the Commission's investigations. Despite this limitation, the knowledge and experience of the group was quite extensive and as well balanced as circumstances would allow.

EVIDENCE PRESENTED TO THE COMMISSION

The Commission notes in its Report on Collective Discrimination that, when the reference was made, five of the Commission's previous reports on individual industries and trades had already dealt with some aspect of the specified practices. The detailed evidence produced by these earlier reports was used by the Commission in its general inquiry. Indeed the Reports themselves had been one of the factors which caused the general reference to be made. The Commission also took account of the evidence supplied in connection with individual industries that were being investigated simultaneously with the general inquiry. It also drew on the evidence of previous committees of inquiry set up in the period 1919-52; for example, the Lloyd Jacob Committee of 1949 had thrown some light on enforcement procedures. The restrictive practices and monopoly legislation of Canada, the U.S.A., Sweden and the Irish Republic was also examined. The bulk of the evidence was, however, provided by the organizations and individuals who operated the specified practices. As the Commission records, many of these people had spent their whole lives in their trade or industry and felt very strongly that their arrangements were in the public interest. In support of this, there is every indication that industrialists co-operated fully in the inquiry and wanted to submit as much evidence as possible to substantiate their case. The Commission made some attempt to canvass the views of industrialists not operating the specified practices, but according to the

Report, this was only found to be possible to a limited extent. This, together with the fact that the consumer viewpoint was difficult to elicit, meant that the Commission found itself unable simply to balance one set of evidence against another. Instead, to use its own words, it had 'to make broad general judgements taking into account both the views of those who have come before us, and our own assessment of the effect of the practices on those who were not in a position to formulate their views so precisely' (p. 12). This does not imply that there were no complaints against the practices, because a number of critical statements were in fact submitted to the Commission—although these came mainly from people who had been excluded from agreements, and would presumably not have been presented if the complainants had been admitted to these.

The question of evidence was particularly relevant, as three members of the group refused to sign the Report on these grounds. Sir Thomas Barnes, Mr. Davidson and Professor Goodhart were not prepared to condemn the specified practices as injurious to the public interest, because they considered that the evidence presented to the Commission did not justify so sweeping a condemnation. As a result of this split, two Conservative M.P.s asked Mr. Thorneycroft to publish the evidence. Mr. Thorneycroft replied that this was not possible owing to the fact that it contained information about the trading position of firms, and was only submitted on the assumption that it would not be published. Also, if the evidence had been published, it would probably have caused industrialists some concern, as some of them were anxious to see the abolition of restrictionism and might have submitted evidence to this effect.

26

THE COMMISSION'S REPORT

The terms of reference for the inquiry were that the Commission should report on the effect on the public interest of certain specified practices. The terms were in fact somewhat restrictive, in that the Commission was charged with investigating the *collective enforcement* of the specified practices, rather than the practices themselves. Thus it could not concern itself with R.P.M. as a principle, but only with its collective enforcement. Similarly, common pricing and level-tendering agreements were excluded from the terms of reference (see Chapter 4). Academic economists have since argued that collective discriminatory trade practices were not logically the best starting point for an inquiry. The collective measures were usually secondary or policing actions designed to secure price-fixing or other selling policies (Brock, 1966). But as is shown in Chapter 4, the collective means of enforcing the policies was a politically convenient and politically necessary starting-point. During its investigations the Commission came across what it termed a bewildering variety of collective agreements falling wholly or in part within the terms of reference of the inquiry. To simplify its work it classified the agreement into six categories, as follows:

1 Collective discrimination by sellers (without any corresponding obligations on the buyers).
2 Collective discrimination by sellers in return for exclusive buying.
3 Collective adoption by sellers of a policy of maintaining resale prices or imposing other collateral trading obligations on the buyers.

4 Collective discrimination by sellers to enforce resale prices or other contract terms.

5 Collective discrimination by buyers.

6 Aggregated rebates.

Conclusions of the majority

The Report considered the effects on the public interest of each of the six categories. The majority of the members of the Commission, while recognizing the differences between the practices, considered that one feature was common to them all. In some way or other they all imposed a collective obligation which of necessity reduced the freedom of the parties to the agreement and therefore had the effect of reducing competition. Consequently, although the majority did not suggest that every single agreement was acting to the public detriment, they nevertheless felt that all the types of agreement that they had examined, affected the public interest adversely in varying degrees. They considered that most of the agreements prevented manufacturers from experimenting with new and perhaps more efficient ways of conducting their businesses, and that they created undue rigidity in industry. They concluded that the 'effect of competition in promoting efficiency and safeguarding the public interest' was greatly reduced where trade was deliberately confined to a particular group of traders (p. 82). This statement goes some way towards explaining the majority's conclusions, as they obviously considered competition to be desirable as a general principle. Having committed themselves in this way it was not surprising that they regarded the specific practices as on the whole undesirable.

Despite this commitment however, the majority were

unwilling to rule out the possibility that some of the agreements could be beneficial.

They listed four criteria which could be used to justify a collective agreement.

1 Were final consumers unable to judge standards of service that it was in their own interests to demand? e.g. safety standards (although they felt that special, separate legislation was needed for this).
2 Was an agreement used to protect industries of strategic economic importance, or an industry subject to dumping? (Though again they felt that this should be covered by special legislation.)
3 Was an agreement necessary to support a common price agreement that could be deemed to be in the public interest?
4 Was an agreement in force to help small firms to compete with large concerns who might themselves be resorting to restrictive practices?

When the Act was finally passed there were in fact seven criteria (or gateways) which industry could plead. The majority also concluded that further legislation was clearly necessary, and therefore suggested two possible alternatives.

(a) To ensure some measure of publicity and supervision, by requiring all agreements within the scope of the reference to be registered, and then to prohibit those which after individual scrutiny were found to be against the public interest.
(b) By Statute to generally prohibit all agreements

covered by the reference, with provision for exceptions in particular cases.

They argued that if the first alternative were adopted, then an independent tribunal should be set up for scrutiny and advice, to which the Minister would refer cases. They rejected this approach on the grounds that further individual review would be of value only in exceptional cases. They therefore came out in favour of their second alternative, i.e. that since in their view the practices were generally against the public interest, then they should be generally banned. They argued that an inquiry should only be instituted where a *prima facie* case had been established under some closely defined criteria. The applications for exemption should be considered by an independent body. It was not proposed that this body should be a decision-taking tribunal—it would advise the Minister, and where he decided to make an exception, this should be effected by means of an order laid before Parliament (p. 87). It is important to note that the Report did not suggest the setting up of a court removed from the responsibility of Parliament, although this was the solution later adopted by the government.

Conclusions of the minority

A minority of the Commission (Sir Thomas Barnes, Mr. Davidson, and Professor Goodhart) disagreed with most of the majority's conclusions. They considered that restriction of competition might in certain circumstances be injurious to the public interest, but they nevertheless concluded that a general prohibition of the agreements would be unfair, and that each industry should have its

30

case examined individually. They therefore favoured the first alternative proposed by the majority, i.e. a system of registration followed by individual examination of cases. The minority, joined by Mr. Gifford, also concluded that the collective enforcement of R.P.M. was not against the public interest. They added that they had no sympathy for the trader who sold below the prescribed price.

Significance of the report

Even before the Report was published, at least one Conservative M.P., at a dinner given by a trade association, had expressed the view that whatever was in the Report was likely to be on the Statute book within a year. This well illustrates the importance of the Report. The various interest groups involved may be said to have lost the battle when they failed to convince the majority of the Commission of their case. The climate of opinion at the time of publication in 1955, was such that the government would have found it extremely difficult to shelve the Report. Hence it was essential for the interest groups that the Report should be favourable to them. Since they had failed to convince a majority of the Commission, when the Bill was being formulated, and during its passage through Parliament, they were always faced with an authoritative condemnation of their activities. The importance of the Report can only be fully appreciated when what may be loosely termed the climate of opinion is considered.

4

The organized interests, public opinion and the press

THE ORGANIZED INTERESTS

The Monopolies Commission Report on Collective Discrimination records that the Commission sent out detailed *questionnaires* to approximately 200 trade associations during its inquiry. Individual concerns and other bodies were also approached, bringing the total number of interests consulted to about 300. The Commission classified these bodies according to the standard industrial classification. The table is reproduced on page 33.

As can be seen from the table only 164 associations supplied detailed statements to the Commission because a number of them did not operate any of the practices under investigation.

The main interests directly involved were industrial trade associations. These generally represent a number of firms which have a common interest in that they manufacture the same product, use the same processes or materials and share the same markets. However, the nature and function of trade associations can vary considerably. For example, the size of the association can

TABLE I Range of the inquiries and statements

Industrial Group	Number of Associations with which we have been in contact	Number of statements describing practices within the reference
Fishing	2	2
Mining and Quarrying	4	—
Non-Metalliferous Manufactures	36	23
Chemicals and Allied Trades	31	9
Pharmaceutical Preparations, Toilet Goods, etc.	9	6
Metal Manufacture	16	11
Engineering	15	6
Electrical Engineering	23	16
Vehicles	10	10
Other Metal Goods	40	26
Precision Instruments, etc.	6	2
Textiles	17	10
Leather and Leather Goods	2	—
Clothing	19	8
Food, Drink and Tobacco	20	11
Wood and Cork	4	—
Paper (including some building materials)	9	7
Printing and Publishing	11	8
Other Manufacturers	16	9
Totals	290	164

Source: Monopolies Commission Report. Cmd. 9504

vary from a handful of firms to thousands of firms, as in the retail associations. Not only is there variation as between different associations, but also marked variations occur within particular associations.

Thus some trade associations may be dominated by one large firm or group of firms and conflicts may arise between the interests of the small and larger firms within the association. This of course raises certain problems of representativeness. For example, can the government be sure that an association is truly representative of its industry? It may in practice represent only the views of the less progressive firms within an industry. The question arises as to whether associations do take up clearly defined positions on particular issues anyway, as they may find it difficult to attain unanimity.

In practice the functions performed by trade associations fall into three categories (P.E.P., 1957).

1 Representative.
2 Common services to improve the efficiency of market knowledge of their members.
3 Maintain devices for purposes of restricting competition.

It is fairly clear that a number of the smaller associations are not particularly efficient in their representative role. Many of the associations have a relatively small staff (very few have more than 100) so that lobbying and the drafting of amendments, etc., does not come easily to them. This is of course not true of the larger industrial associations which are very skilled indeed in their representative role. However, the fact that there are a large number of industrial trade associations with very small bureaucracies,

34

means that what Professor Finer has termed the 'peak associations' (Finer, 1966, 9) become extremely important when legislation is introduced which affects industry as a whole. This was particularly true in 1955-6 when the three peak associations in existence at the time (F.B.I., N.U.M., and A.B.C.C.) played the leading role in presenting industry's case to government and parliament.

As well as industrial trade associations, certain wholesale and retail associations were also very concerned with the problem, particularly where it involved the collective enforcement of R.P.M. For example the Proprietary Articles Trade Association and a body called the Fair Prices Defence Committee were associations very closely concerned with the defence of the practice. Such associations tended to exert influence independently of the larger peak associations. The local authority associations and the Co-operative societies were also interested, the former because they were often at the receiving end of the practices in question, as large purchasers, and the latter because their dividend policy was often considered by manufacturers to be a breach of R.P.M. conditions. Both the local authority associations and the Co-operative movement, as large consumers, tended to be against restrictive practices although they were the only organized groups to take this attitude. It would therefore be wrong to describe the situation in 1955-6 as one of group conflict, though as will be indicated in Chapter 5, pressure from local authority associations was almost certainly influential in instituting the Monopolies Commission Inquiry.

PUBLIC OPINION

It is sometimes suggested that pressure groups may con-

35

stitute a threat to parliamentary government if their power increases. If this is a real possibility then public opinion and the press may act as a safeguard. It is of course difficult to define what is meant by the term public opinion at any point in time. This does not however preclude the possibility of assessing its likely influence at a given time. The question immediately arises as to how public opinion manages to express itself. As the public is not organized it remains an ill-defined mass containing a multitude of conflicting opinions. It is true that the public contains a number of well-organized groups which perform the essential function of transmitting the various viewpoints to the government, but nevertheless the majority of voters remain unorganized and as a result their voice is diffused.

The Monopolies Commission was particularly handicapped by this factor during its inquiries. It commented that it was extremely difficult to seek the views of consumers 'partly because few consumers could speak in any representative capacity and partly because few were sufficiently informed of the arrangements in particular trades to be able to assess their general effects'. In fact one of the reasons for the minority's Report was that few complaints had been received from the public concerning the practices. But despite this, the minority recognized what they termed the public uneasiness on the matter, although they attributed this concern to the use of what had been termed the Star Chamber methods by certain trade associations.

Members of Parliament may perhaps be in a better position than most to judge public feeling on an issue, although they are unlikely to obtain any truly representative sample of opinion. During the various debates in the House of Commons on monopoly and restrictive practices it was quite common for M.P.s to refer to the size of the mail which they had received complaining about restrictive practices. The speeches made by M.P.s indicated that there was a certain degree of public concern. Their assessment was probably correct, however ill-defined this concern was. But even if the public was not concerned or interested in the problem it is significant that a number of M.P.s, civil servants and members of the government thought it was and they reacted accordingly.

THE PRESS

We must turn to the attitude of the press to provide much of the explanation of the likely influence of public opinion. The press itself felt that some concern did exist in the public mind. For example *The Observer*, early in 1955, commented that what it considered to be the government's complacent attitude to price fixing and restrictive practices in industry and trade, would not help the Conservatives in the impending general election. The *Daily Express* thought that private enterprise had less to fear from Communists than from the irresponsible recklessness of the price fixers. *The Financial Times* also reported that the government was soon to make an effort to control monopolies and restrictive practices which were becoming immediate political issues. *The Economist*, even though it was sceptical of the public's attitude, felt that the Monopolies Commission Report would serve as a useful instrument to heat up public opinion, though it still maintained that public opinion was not really prepared for anything more than an attack on certain practices that it had been told (usually wrongly) were the

37

worst ones. (The problems concerning both monopoly and restrictive practices are in reality so complex that it would be rather surprising if the general public could fully comprehend the issues involved.)

Trade association courts

In 1955 and 1956 however, certain events occurred which dramatized the issues involved as far as the popular press was concerned and, through its influence, the public as well. A good example of this is the case of a motor-accessory dealer in Stockport who was tried in the private court of his trade association and was charged with selling goods below the list price. This was of course nothing new. What was new was that the dealer concerned fought the case and the press reported it widely. Thus a headline in the *Daily Mail* read 'Price Ring Courts Carry On— Motor Dealer Tried for Third Time' (9 July 1955). When the dealer's case was first reported all the popular news-papers gave his story considerable prominence, and all came out against the practice of having private courts to try members for breach of trade association rules. The *Daily Express* described the case as an intolerable affront to justice. The *News Chronicle* headlined its story 'Black Listed—He Takes 10 per cent off Profit'. A few days earlier the *Daily Express* had reported the case of a barber also of Stockport, who had been similarly tried for cutting hair below the agreed association price. Earlier in 1955 it had also published an article headed 'Why you pay £20 for tubes that cost £4' (15 March 1955) and explained that the reason for this was that a price ring existed in the television tube industry.

The general assessment of public opinion was very

much of this nature, i.e. that great injustices were being perpetrated behind closed doors (the fact that the evocative term Star Chamber became the popular description of the trade association courts is indicative of this). In many ways the press itself was more concerned with this aspect of the problem than with its true economic significance. The *Daily Mail*, for example, declared that it did not intend to argue the ethics of price maintenance, but nevertheless felt that the public must view with alarm the way in which the trader was tried and found guilty. The case of the Stockport dealer was by no means unique. Other cases which were given extensive publicity concerned motor dealers selling tyres at cut prices to people who turned out to be what Harold Wilson described as snoopers for trade associations. The case of a trader in Birmingham whose supplies of tea were withheld because he had sold it at cut price to old-age pensioners also roused public feeling. The general public, faced with reports of such cases in the popular press, inevitably became antagonistic towards trade associations.

Level tendering

A second issue, that of level tendering, also led to widespread press comment in 1955. This practice (often called collusive tendering) consisted of all firms in an association agreeing to submit the same tender for a given contract. At least 25 cases of this were reported in the latter half of 1955. Practically every newspaper carried a report of each case as it arose, often with headlines that were as dramatic as those concerning the operation of private trade association courts. In June 1955, for example, Bristol City Corporation received identical tenders for a quantity of cement. As the issue had become one of Labour's points of attack on the government, the *Daily Herald*, naturally enough headlined its report 'City Held to Ransom'. At the other end of the political spectrum, the *Daily Express* bluntly stated '14 Tenders *All* the Same'. The same sort of treatment had been given to earlier reports of identical tenders being received for steelwork for a school in West Hartlepool. The *News Chronicle* headed its story 'Kill the Price Rings Says Education Chief'. The *Daily Express*, commenting on the increasing number of cases of price fixing and level tendering, regarded the Monopolies Commission as feeble and called for a vigorous attack on the price rings. In June 1955 the *News Chronicle* reported that the government had been considering the matter urgently as a result of the feeling aroused by recent cases. By October 1955 the government had decided to refer the practice of level tendering and common prices to the Commission as a second reference under section 15 of the 1948 Act. This reference, made on 29 October 1955, was originally termed 'Common Prices and Collusive Tendering'. However, after certain representations, the government modified the wording of the reference substituting the word 'level' for 'collusive'. It is fairly evident that this new reference to the Commission was a direct result of the campaign conducted in the press and in Parliament against these practices. Quite apart from all this the Board of Trade had also received a deputation from the Association of Municipal Corporations complaining about the effects of level tendering.

The appearance of the Monopolies Commission Report on Collective Discrimination reinforced any feelings that existed against restrictive practices and provided, as we have seen in Chapter 3, a great deal of evidence for those wishing to attack the use of such practices. The Commission's findings were widely reported in, and welcomed by, the popular press. Typical of the reception accorded by the press was that of the *Daily Express* which considered the Report to be a vigorous blow by the Commission at the abuses which it had been set up to correct. The quality or opinion-leader newspapers also adopted this attitude. *The Financial Times* carried the headline 'Trade Practices Condemned—Private Courts Against Public Interest'. *The Times* thought that the government should act at least on the recommendations of the Minority Report, and considered that even the Majority Report, though perhaps in too great a hurry, was heading in the right direction.

The publication of the Report forced the government into the position of having to take some action. It would have been very difficult to shelve it. The decision to make a general reference to the Commission in 1952 might have succeeded in temporarily shelving the issue (if that had been the government's intention) but when the Report was completed, not only were the majority quite plain in their conclusions, but it was also published amid a growing demand for action on the part of the press generally. The critical press attitude continued in 1956. The *Daily Express* had at one time considered Mr. Thorneycroft's attitude to the Commission's Report as being both timid and trivial, but in January 1956, it reported that the Minister had turned tough and as a result intended to stiffen the forthcoming legislation. It warmly welcomed this change in attitude.

When the Bill (described in Chapter 5) was introduced it was fairly well received although the *Daily Mail* expressed a commonly held doubt about the wisdom of setting up a judicial court to deal with the problem. It concluded wisely that the attitude of the court in practice would turn out to be the deciding factor. *The Economist's* first reaction was to be thankful that a Conservative government had introduced such a Bill at all. It too was somewhat suspicious of the decision to set up a court, and expressed the hope that the new court should be as liberal as the Commission had been. It also criticized the seven gateways in the Bill, the increased powers of individual enforcement of R.P.M., and the reduction in the size of the Monopolies Commission. *The Times* felt that public opinion and the government had rightly concluded that competition had been excessively restricted in Britain, that there must be more of it and that the common law on restraint of trade was quite inadequate to secure it. It shared *The Economist's* doubt about some of the gateways in the Bill. *The Guardian* thought the Bill was a bold measure by any political test (which it probably was), but criticized the strengthening of individual R.P.M. The quality press or opinion-leader newspapers had all at various times called for action against restrictionism and all cautiously welcomed the government's policy when introduced. The decision to abolish the collective enforcement of R.P.M. (and as a result the system of private courts behind it) was particularly welcomed by the popular press as this seemed to meet much of their earlier criticism.

The influence of press and public opinion

What then can be concluded from the above description of the attitude of the press? There is certainly no direct relationship between the press coverage of an issue and the degree of public concern associated with it. Their interrelations are complex to say the least. Wide press coverage may mean that the press itself believes the public to be concerned about a given issue. As we have seen, a number of newspapers certainly felt that this was the case with private trade courts and the practice of level tendering. On the other hand the press may itself *create* opinion simply by reporting an issue widely in a particular way. However, it is probable that any attempt by policy makers to assess the state of opinion in 1955/6 would have produced a firm response in favour of action. Thus as Professor Rose has suggested 'occasionally, deliberations take place in circumstances in which awareness of popular preferences (whether or not correctly perceived) dominate the situation' (Rose, 1965, 210). One cannot argue that policy-makers' perceptions of popular preferences *dominated* the situation as so many factors combined and interacted in this example of the policy process. But it is fair to conclude that public opinion and the attitude of the press was an important input in the process. Henry Brooke, as Minister of Housing in 1958, seems to have been confronted by a similar situation which led him to modify certain provisions in the 1957 Rent Act. Mr. Brooke's change in attitude has been attributed by Ronald Butt to criticism of the effects of the Act by the press so that 'Brooke began to see that he faced a possible press campaign built upon the personal stories of dispossessed elderly tenants' (Butt, 1967, 219).

In 1955/6 the government was receiving a very bad press on the issue of restrictive practices and the Labour Opposition was making political capital out of this discontent. In this way public opinion can be said to have played an influential role in the policy process. This conclusion

43

has also been put forward by Sir David Cairns who, in commenting on the Restrictive Trade Practices Act, suggests that the singling out of stop lists and private courts for prohibition was a victory for the opinions of the general public and the press (Ginsberg, 1959, 192). This of course is not to suggest that the press and public opinion influenced the important features of the Bill as introduced, for there was doubt, as *The Economist* suggested at the time, as to whether the public understood the real issue. The public's technical ignorance and its preoccupation with the moral issue considerably weakened its influence on the detailed statutory reforms and consequently helped the organized interests to gain important concessions in the proposed legislation.

5

The Board of Trade and the contents of the Bill

The Board of Trade in 1955/6 was the most important of the departments concerned with trade and industry. Besides being concerned with matters of trade and industry generally, the Board was also concerned specifically with the problem of monopolies and restrictive practices.

Under the terms of the Monopolies and Restrictive Practices (Inquiry and Control) Act, 1948, the Board of Trade had been given both the function of selecting cases for reference to the Monopolies Commission, and in many cases of acting on the Reports of the Commission. In practice the Board was not the only government department responsible for taking actions on Reports. The production department of the industry concerned was, under the terms of the 1948 Act, responsible for taking any action deemed necessary. For example, the Dental Goods Order was made by the Minister of Health as the responsible authority. Specific questions relating to individual Reports were not necessarily addressed to the President of the

Board of Trade but to the Minister of the relevant department. This division of responsibility between various ministers caused some criticism. It was argued that a uniform co-ordinated policy was difficult to achieve if six or seven departments had some responsibility for enforcing policy. There seems little justification for this criticism if account is taken of the manner in which the government has implemented the Commission's recommendations. This has been largely a matter of negotiating with the industry or firm concerned, in order to reach agreement on how the recommendations accepted by the government should be carried out. Since it is the sponsoring department's job to be aware of the broad lines of production policy and general market conditions in the industry which it covers, it is readily understandable in terms of administrative efficiency that any major dealings with a particular industry are best carried out by the department which is most familiar with it.

Criteria for selecting references

The Board of Trade's main function up to 1956, was that of making references to the Commission and implementing certain of the recommendations accepted by the government and can be seen to be of considerable importance. It used four basic criteria in selecting references to the Commission (see Board of Trade Annual Report on the Working of the Act, 1953, 5).

1 The nature of the trades and practices covered by matters already investigated by the Commission.
2 The size of the trade and its importance in the national economy.

46

3 The volume and the nature of the representations received concerning the effect of conditions or practices in that trade.
4 The possibility that an inquiry into a particular matter might (a) yield conclusions capable of wide application or (b) might serve as a pilot test for indicating whether inquiries into other problems of a similar kind might be useful.

Representations to the Board

The terms of the 1948 Act provided for the Board to receive suggestions, complaints and recommendations from persons or bodies affected by restrictive practices and monopolies. Provision was also made for the publication of the names of persons making the complaint if the person so desired. This latter provision was rarely invoked, although in 1951 the Municipal Transport Association is recorded as having suggested that the Monopolies Commission should inquire into the pricing of tyres. Other bodies mentioned as having made suggestions include the Urban District Councils' Association, the Parliamentary Committee of the Co-operative Society and the Municipal Corporations Association. The majority of the suggestions were listed anonymously in the Board's report. This caused some bitterness in industry in that it was sometimes suggested that industries were being judged on evidence to which they had no access. When questioned on this point during an Estimates Committee investigation in 1953, the Chairman of the Monopolies Commission replied that ninety-five per cent of its judgements were made on evidence supplied by the industry itself.

47

It is beyond doubt that the Board of Trade received many suggestions and requests. Some forty goods and services were recorded in the First Annual Report alone. These covered a very wide range—from a complaint that a monopoly existed in the supply of spinning machinery, to a suggestion that a restrictive association operated in the monumental masonry trade. By 1955 the Board had received over 150 suggestions and complaints of this nature (this figure represents different goods and services—in many cases the same suggestions were repeated year after year). The Board was of course free to go outside the list of suggestions and requests from the public. Although some of the suggestions were clearly not suitable for investigation, the Board was faced with a great deal of *prima facie* evidence on restrictionism.

Evidence of restrictionism

The question of whether sufficient evidence was available, is very relevant because this was a bone of contention for many years. This question always arose when the problem dealing with monopolistic tendencies in British industry was debated. In this context it is worth noting that apart from representations made to it, the Board must have been aware of the problem through its contact with government purchasing departments. Since large purchasing organizations like local authorities had become increasingly aware of the existence and effects of restrictionism, then it is clear that the government departments themselves must have had a great deal of information, as they are amongst the largest purchasers in Britain. Evidence to support this is provided by a letter sent by the Board in 1965 to all principal organizations representing

British industry. This letter revealed that the government had instructed all its departments to help uncover hidden price rings and other restrictive practices. The evidence of the Report by Political and Economic Planning points in the same direction. This states that 'The contracting department may be faced with a tight price ring and it may be necessary for them to enter discussions with the organization concerned' (P.E.P., 1957, 93). This awareness of the problem influenced the Board's attitude when the time came to draft the 1956 Bill, and when the process of consultation was carried out.

It is interesting to note just how little the general public entered into the work of the Board. On many occasions the Board's Annual Reports refer to the marked lack of representations from the general body of consumers in Britain. Thus for example, the 1951 Report observed that the majority of suggestions had come from business people who considered that their competitive position had been impaired. The practice which gave rise to the greatest number of complaints was that in which the association of suppliers agreed to sell only to an approved list of persons, or to grant special terms to persons on an approved list. It is clear that the volume and nature of representations received was influential in determining the terms of reference of the Monopoly Commission's general inquiry set up in 1952. The only true consumer interests to make representations to the Board were the local authority associations. Their representations were very strong concerning common-price systems and level tendering. The results of a *questionnaire* sent out by the County Councils' Association in 1954 to its members showed that these practices were common in many basic materials used by highway departments.

49

The attitude and influence of the Board: a case of role conflict

The delay in the implementation of the Monopolies Commission recommendations often caused the Board of Trade to be seriously criticized, so much so in fact that the Board gained the reputation for being the second best ear-stroker in the country. Thus D. H. Robertson has said that

> There is a saying in England—that there are two ways of getting a donkey to move along a road—by holding a carrot in front of his nose, and by applying a stick to his behind, but experts say there is also a third way of which we normally hear less—namely by stroking his ears; in other words by establishing a code by means of which the animal becomes aware of what is expected of him and he behaves accordingly (Robertson, 1956, 155).

He added that it was not unduly cynical to question the wisdom of relying permanently on the operation of this system over such a large and controversial field, and wondered if this were putting too much strain on human nature. Similarly, Mackenzie and Grove (1957, 248) have stated that it is not easy for a department to urge industry on the one hand to combine in effective association, yet on the other to take on the job of dealing with trade associations which go too far.

These comments well illustrate the invidious and difficult position in which the Board of Trade found itself in the early 1950s. We have noted in an earlier chapter that the government had often encouraged the growth and formation of representative associations, and the Board and all government departments are certainly well aware that they have to rely on trade associations for a great deal of technical information. As a result, contacts between civil servants and trade associations are very frequent. For example, it has been estimated that a number of Assistant Secretaries in the production departments, spend half their time on matters involving liaison with trade associations. It is clear that if a department such as this were to be responsible for a policy opposed by the majority of trade associations, then a certain degree of friction and embarrassment would have been caused.

Refusing to co-operate with the government is generally regarded as the last resort of pressure groups. However, the dividing line between co-operation and non-co-operation is not at all clear cut (Finer, 1966, 26). When day-to-day contact between industrialists and civil servants is so common, bitterness or ill-feeling can reduce the efficiency of the working relationship rather drastically. The Board of Trade certainly enjoyed good relations with industry up to 1956. As evidence of this, the British Electrical and Allied Manufacturers' Association commented in its Annual Report for 1955/6 that the Board at all times did its utmost to assist B.E.A.M.A. officials to promote the welfare of the industry. This close and indeed very useful relationship between the Board and industry is of great significance when the controversy over what type of tribunal should judge restrictive practices is considered. The evidence of widespread restrictionism, together with the Monopolies Commission Report confirming this, meant that the Board tended to favour an attack on restrictive agreements. There was, however, a feeling in industry that this was not strictly fair on the part of the Board, and that indeed it was stabbing industry in the back. Therefore it was understandable that the Board was anxious to avoid the unpleasant task of enforcing any strong anti-restrictionist policy. This anxiety inclined the Board towards the judicial solution that was so strongly favoured by industry. Handing over the problem to an independent court of law meant that the Board could hope to avoid the bitter criticism from industrialists, and yet at the same time increase competition. Thus although the Board itself favoured action, its views may well have strengthened the influence of the organized interests on this particular issue.

A general ideology?

Fears that the Board of Trade had developed a general ideology which made it unsuited to play an interventionist role in industry, led in part to the Labour party's decision to set up the Department of Economic Affairs in 1964. According to M. Shanks, the party rejected the idea of the Board as a super-ministry of industry, partly because of the Board's 'unfortunate history' in the late fifties and early sixties (Shanks, 1967, 110). He argues that the Board, believing firmly in *laissez-faire*, was distrustful of Neddy (N.E.D.C.) and other innovations and was fearful of becoming the target for protectionist lobbies in industry and therefore remained out of the swim. He concludes that the Board was generally unwilling to assume a more positive and interventionist role in industry. Shanks also seems to recognize the dangers of too close a relationship between Whitehall and trade associations and sees this as an argument for the Economic Development Committees since these are set apart from the established channels 'where the wealth of vested interests must inevitably be great'

(Shanks, 1967, 130). Similarly, Samuel Brittan has argued that the habit of asking lawyers and other outsiders to make judgements on essentially *political* issues (like wages and restrictive practices), illustrates just how badly the machinery of government was working (Brittan, 1964, 304). This reluctance to intervene has been described by A. Shonfield as being part of the traditional ideology in Britain which continued to assert its influence even in the post-war period (Shonfield, 1965). He says that this ideology is illustrated by the refusal of ministers to plan, and by the administrative devices invented for them by civil servants. To quote Shonfield, the civil servants 'were anxious above all to ensure that the exercise of new powers of government did not saddle them with the responsibility of making choices for which later they might be accountable' (Shonfield, 1965, 94). In his view, the typical British civil servant particularly dislikes the job of discriminating between businessmen, and that of handing out rewards and penalties.

The fact that the Board was not anxious to take on this particular interventionist job of handing out penalties to restrictive trade associations, lends considerable support to these views. Also, even as late as 1960, the Board seemed quite satisfied with the Restrictive Practices Court as a piece of controlling machinery. When asked by the Chairman of the Estimates Committee whether he had any reason for being disappointed at the speed with which it worked, Sir Frank Lee (Permanent Secretary Board of Trade 1951-59) replied that in his view it had been a very effective piece of machinery. Further indication of the Board's attitude came in 1966 when it had to negotiate with the petrol companies about the Commission's report on their industry. Thus, according to *The Sunday Times*

53

(12 June 1966), the major petrol companies succeeded in extracting major concessions from the Board.

THE 1956 BILL

The Bill was introduced into the House of Commons on 15 February 1956. Its main provisions were as follows:

(1) It provided for the registration by a Registrar of Restrictive Trading Agreements, of an extensive category of agreements. It also provided for their *judicial* examination by a special court, to be called the Restrictive Practices Court. It further provided for the prohibition of those agreements found to be against the public interest.

(2) It prohibited outright the collective enforcement of resale price maintenance, although the powers of the *individual* trader to enforce the price of his goods were increased (he was given power to take legal proceedings against traders who cut prices).

The Bill was divided into three sections which are briefly outlined below.

Part I: registration and judicial investigation on agreements

Clause 1. This provided for the appointment by Her Majesty, of a Registrar of Restrictive Trading Agreements who was to keep the register and take proceedings in respect of agreements before the Court. The Board of Trade was given the power to determine the order in which agreements should be taken.

Clauses 2, 3 and 4. These provided for the establishment of a new Court of Record to be called the Restrictive

54

Practices Court. It was to consist of five judges and not more than nine other members appointed from persons 'having knowledge of, or experience in industry, commerce or public affairs'. It was to be allowed to sit in two or more divisions concurrently.

Clauses 5 and 6. These described the agreements to which Part I applies. They were agreements between persons carrying on business as producers, processors or suppliers of goods within the U.K. (or associations composed of such persons). Under these agreements, mutual restrictions were accepted concerning prices, terms and conditions of trading, quantities or descriptions of goods, areas or places of trading, and persons with whom business might be carried out. The clauses also covered recommendations by trade associations to their members, not explicitly restrictive. Certain exceptions were defined in the clauses, two of which were agreements relating exclusively to exports and agreements relating to wages, hours and conditions of work.

Clause 7. This provided for the registration of the restrictive agreements. The Board of Trade by an order subject to Parliamentary approval, was to determine the dates on which certain classes of agreement were to be registered.

Clause 8. This outlined the particulars which parties had to give the Registrar, and provided him with powers to secure a High Court order directing that the particulars be furnished.

Clauses 9 and 10. These defined the form and contents of the register. It was to be open to public inspection, apart

55

from a special section which would contain particulars that it was not in the public interest to publish.

Clause 11. This gave the Registrar powers to obtain all the information he required. It also gave him the power to enter and search premises.

Clauses 12 and 13. These defined the offences in connection with failing to register an agreement, and defined the penalties attached.

Clause 14. This defined the powers of the Registrar to make regulations for the purpose of registration.

Clauses 15 to 18. These defined the jurisdiction, powers and procedure of the Court. The Court was given the power to decide whether or not registered agreements were against the public interest. It was also given the power to make an order preventing other agreements to the like effect. The Court's jurisdiction was to be brought into play at the request of the Registrar. The onus of proving to the Court that the restrictions were not contrary to public interest was placed on the parties to the agreement. Agreements were deemed to be contrary to the public interest, unless it could be shown by the parties to an agreement that it satisfied at least one of the specific tests or *gateways* as they were later called. The gateways were defined in Clause 16 and were as follows:
(a) that the restriction was reasonably necessary for the protection of the public in connection with the purchase, consumption, installation or use of goods requiring special knowledge or skill;
(b) that the removal of the restriction would deny the

56

public other substantial benefits or advantages;

(c) that the restriction was reasonably necessary to counteract measures taken by other persons not party to the agreement, which prevented competition;

(d) that the restriction was reasonably necessary to enable the parties to negotiate fair terms with persons controlling a large part of the trade;

(e) that the restriction was reasonably necessary to enable the parties to comply with the terms of the Income Tax Act, 1952;

(f) that the restriction prevented serious and persistent unemployment in an area in which a substantial proportion of the trade was situated or that abandonment of the agreement would cause a substantial reduction in the volume or earnings of the U.K. export trade;

(g) that the restriction was reasonably necessary to maintain another restriction not contrary to the public interest. These clauses also declared that the agreements, apart from passing one of the above specified tests, had to be shown not to be detrimental to the public. (This was commonly termed the 'tailpiece' to what was eventually to become Section 21 in the final Act.)

Part II: resale price maintenance

Clauses 19 and 20. These prohibited agreements by suppliers and recommendations by their associations to discriminate against dealers who refused to observe R.P.M. conditions. The same applied to discrimination by dealers. The clauses enabled the individual supplier to enforce the price of his goods through the Courts.

Part III : amendments to the Monopolies and Restrictive Practices Act 1948 and 1953

Clauses 22 and 23. These provided for the reconstruction of the Monopolies and Restrictive Practices Commission (re-named the Monopolies Commission). The membership was to be reduced from a maximum of twenty-five to a maximum of ten. The agreements registered under the 1956 Act were to be excluded from the jurisdiction of the Commission.

Clause 24. This removed the power of the competent authority to make orders (under Section 10 of the 1948 Act) concerned with practices included in the terms of the 1956 Act.

Clause 25. This excluded export agreements from the terms of the Act, but the particulars of the agreements were to be furnished to the Board of Trade.

The contents of the Bill must be judged against some scale of possibilities. At one end of this scale we may place total prohibition of the restrictive practices which had been investigated by the Commission, plus prohibition of level tendering and common prices. This solution may be termed a strong solution. At the other end of the scale (a weak solution), we may place the possibility of the maintenance of the status quo by the government. The proposals of the majority of the Commission would fall just short of the top end of the scale, as they proposed that some *prima facie* exceptions should be allowed (although in fact they did not come across any in their investigations). The minority proposals would fall in the lower half of the scale, as they suggested the registration of agreements followed by individual examination. Where then does the Government's Bill lie on such a scale? The answer would seem to be somewhere in the middle. Total prohibition was not accepted and in fact the solution did involve the individual examination of cases, after registration. However, the Bill is stronger than the minority proposals in that the terms under which examination of each case was to take place, were fairly closely defined in clause 16 (even though it has often been argued that clause 16 was too weak). The Bill also banned collective enforcement of R.P.M. But (as will be shown in the next chapter), despite all this, the Bill contained many proposals in line with the representations which the Government had received.

6

The role of the organized interests and the position of the Government

It is commonly argued that pressure groups, particularly those of a sectional nature, are generally concerned with the politics of detail rather than the politics of issues (Stewart, 1958, 29). The argument behind this assumption is that groups realize that they are unlikely to change the contents of a Bill in principle, and can only hope to gain concessions on the detailed contents and application of the Government's policy. The evidence provided by this case study supports this assertion. However, an important qualification must be made, in that it is often difficult to decide whether or not a concession is a mere detail or whether in practice, and at a later date, it may turn out to be of much greater importance. This is particularly the case with the 1956 Act. As we shall see in Chapter 8, it is now believed that many loopholes exist in the Act, which were apparently not obvious at the time. As a result, many observers argue that the Act is not as effective in increasing competition as it could be. The reason for this may well be that an accumulation of detailed concessions and amendments may, added together, significantly blunt the intentions of the framers of legislation.

An excellent example of a so-called detailed concession is an amendment proposed by the A.B.C.C., F.B.I. and N.U.M., relieving industry of the task of proving an absence of harm to the public. In practice there is a great difference between, on the one hand, balancing any benefits from an agreement against any proven detriments, and, on the other, proving the *absence* of any detriment, as the Bill had originally intended. Although *The Economist* described this amendment as a detailed concession, this was not the attitude adopted by the individuals directly affected by the legislation. The industrialists had all along complained that the Bill as originally drafted placed a burden of negative proof on them. For example, the A.B.C.C., in its press statement in March 1956, complained that this duty had been 'quite unfairly placed on industry, which has not the information necessary to discharge it, and cannot be expected to disprove charges not formulated against it'.

The basis of influence

The structure of the interests involved has been outlined in a previous chapter. How then did they attempt to influence the policy process? As Professor Finer argues (Finer, 1966, 110), the Lobby always attempts to convince the government that concessions are not only in the interest of the Lobby but serve the public interest as well. Somehow the government, Parliament and the Ministry concerned have to be persuaded that this is so. Alternatively the Lobby has to show the government that concessions are in the government's own *political* interest, irrespective of public interest considerations. In this case at least three factors helped the industrial interests to influence government policy. Firstly, communication with policy makers was excellent. The groups concerned did not have to establish links with civil servants or M.P.s because the links were already in existence. As we have seen, trade associations had very close ties with the Board of Trade, so that the individuals concerned were already used to working with each other. Similarly many Conservative backbenchers were members or even officeholders of various trade associations. Thus an important basis of persuasion—the personal contact—was very much in evidence in 1955/6. Secondly, the latent threat of group sanctions was certainly a possibility in this case. This is not to say that the groups concerned did actually threaten to use sanctions in order to gain concessions. Nevertheless the strategic economic position of the groups must have helped them to an important degree. Much of the efficient application of government policy in the industrial field depends on the co-operation of industry. Clearly anyone contemplating any legislative action in this field has to bear this in mind. As we have seen, the attitude of the Board of Trade seems to lend support to this suggestion, even though the groups did not adopt an aggressive attitude. A third basis of persuasion is that of informed argument, as pressure groups are often an essential source of information. This is particularly true of industrial trade associations and the groups were able to deploy well-documented arguments to support their case. However, the extent to which 'good arguments' could be used as a basis of persuasion in 1955/6 was limited in that the Monopolies Commission had already examined most of the arguments and had, on balance, rejected them. Also, parliamentary, press and public criticism had created a difficult situation for the groups concerned, but the groups still managed to ensure that their arguments were very effectively voiced.

The representation of interests

The three 'peak associations' played by far the most important role in this attempt to influence the policy process. The bulk of the influence exerted by trade and industry was channelled through the A.B.C.C., F.B.I. and N.U.M., or through the joint committee which they eventually formed to deal with the passage of the Bill. [The F.B.I. and N.U.M. have since merged and together with the British Employers' Confederation now form the Confederation of British Industry.] In fact all trade associations, and also the peak organizations, found some difficulty in making representations as they all represented diverse and often conflicting interests. Certain sections of British industry were anxious to see some kind of legislation to remove restrictive practices. For example, the industrial correspondent of *The Times*, in May 1955, argued that in private (though not in public) industrialists were divided in their attitude to monopoly and restrictive practices. Some of the most distinguished industrial leaders believed that restrictive agreements reduced the size of their own business and fostered the growth of firms who were less efficient and who did less research. Reports of Anglo-U.S. productivity teams also indicated that some industrialists were irritated by certain of the restraints placed upon them by the British trade association system. Therefore in 1956 the task of peak organizations like the F.B.I. was by no means an easy one. In the same way, in 1964 many

63

industrialists were in favour of the abolition of R.P.M., but were not prepared to take active steps to end it, as they were under some pressure from their colleagues to close ranks in defence of R.P.M. Now that two of the peak organizations have merged, the task of representation will become increasingly difficult. The formation of a new group, the Society of Independent Manufacturers, which is a body designed to represent the interests of the small- and medium-sized firm, suggests that the problems of maintaining cohesion have not decreased. The government encourages the formation of large-scale umbrella organizations as this makes the system of consultation much simpler from their point of view. On the other hand the efficacy of the consultations may be impaired if the organizations consulted find difficulty in reducing the multitude of opinions into one authoritative voice of industry. In many ways such organizations function like political parties, i.e. they act as unifiers. The process of conflict resolution within these bodies deserves further study.

Informed argument

Even though divisions existed within industry in 1955/6, the organized interest remained very active. Any attempt to influence public opinion would have had to be on a very large scale because of the adverse climate of opinion which surrounded the use of restrictive agreements. It is also questionable whether such campaigns ever meet with real success. To a great extent there was little need to mobilize public support because more important channels of communication were open to the groups. The tendency was for the smaller retail associations to make far more noise than the industrial associations. The techniques used by the

A.B.C.C., F.B.I. and N.U.M. and their constituent associations were generally silent and relatively unobserved. This difference in approach stems from the fact that the industrial associations are relatively more important and have better access to policy makers. Even so, however, the views of the peak industrial associations were well known and publicized in 1955 and 1956, although they in no way mounted a publicity campaign as such. The F.B.I. was the first to publish its views in 1955, before the Monopolies Commission produced its report. Its pamphlet attempted to give a summary of the views of industry, and to set out all the relevant arguments. The policy recommendations were rather vague, reflecting the division which existed in industry. As Professor Potter has argued, when there is serious disagreement 'the result is at most a very general statement of policy' (Potter, 1961, 115). Similarly, in 1949, the Federation failed to produce any scheme for consumer protection because divergence within itself was too great, with the result that it could only collect the opinions of individual trade associations (Finer, S. E., 'The F.B.I.,' *Political Studies*, iv [1956] 63).

The main argument contained in the pamphlet in 1955 was that it was impossible to generalize about restrictive practices and that as a result it was essential that each case should be judged on its merits. The Federation considered that the investigation of individual cases by an independent tribunal was the correct approach. Also, it argued, various factors limited the adverse effects of restrictive practices. There was always competition from raw materials and foreign competition at home and abroad. All consumer goods competed with each other for the consumer's purse. Large buyers and groups of buyers exercised a considerable bargaining power in their own right. In

65

addition the practices were claimed to have various beneficial effects. They enabled firms to provide for the future.
They ensured orderly adaptation to change and a regular
output so that the firm could plan ahead. They helped the
small firm to keep active and independent, as well as
increasing exports and efficiency. Individual and collective
enforcement of R.P.M. was also defended. The contents of
the pamphlet were widely reported in the press, though
editorial comment was not altogether favourable. The
News Chronicle, for example, was critical of the Federation's generalizations and considered that the pamphlet
failed to shed more specialized light on the problem.

The N.U.M. (later to become the N.A.B.M.) published
its memorandum in 1955, though this was after the publication of the Monopolies Commission Report and after
some of the government intentions had been made known.
The memorandum called for a judicial rather than an
administrative tribunal and argued that the tribunal itself
should not act as prosecutor. It advocated that practices
should be assumed to be unobjectionable until they had
individually been proved contrary to the public interest.
This memorandum, like that of the F.B.I., received wide
coverage in the press and was followed in November 1955
by a published letter sent to Mr. Thorneycroft. This letter
included a statement that no definition of the public interest should be attempted, and suggested that the tribunal
should be left to hear all the evidence and should 'decide
on balance which way the evidence lay'. It argued that the
tribunal should make its judgements in the light of judicial
precedent. We can see the significance of this last point
if reference is made to the judicial decisions made in this
field over the last fifty years.

During 1955 the A.B.C.C. also produced a widely publicized statement which was sent to Mr. Thorneycroft and Members of Parliament. It is instructive to note that it included a plea for any legislation to include restrictive practices and arrangements of organized labour as well. The Association, in its Annual Report for 1955/6, considered that the introduction of this argument 'was not without its effect on parliamentary and public opinion' and that it certainly conditioned the atmosphere in which the Bill was debated in Parliament. However, although some Conservative backbenchers, and indeed the Minister, made repeated reference to restrictive practices on the part of labour (and the nationalized industries), there was little likelihood of these being included under the new legislation. *The Observer*, supporting this view, commented that the Bill, when eventually introduced, was too weak for any attack on the trade unions to be possible. Whether or not the Association's claim is justified is difficult to determine. It definitely did not dissuade many trade unions from passing resolutions in favour of an attack on trade association restrictions, and did not deter the official Opposition from criticizing the Bill. The Association, like the F.B.I., was anxious to point out that it was dangerous to generalize about restrictive trading agreements. It was basically against widespread registration of the agreements. The A.B.C.C.'s statement was also particularly emphatic about the type of tribunal, and considered the form of the tribunal to be the most important single factor in ensuring that the judgements were fair. It argued that a judicial tribunal appointed by the Lord Chancellor was essential. Such a tribunal should consist of judges and also two or three members appointed for their knowledge and experience of industry and commerce. A panel of 'assessors' (experts in particular industries) should be appointed

67

to advise the tribunal. It was further proposed that, instead of widespread registration, the Board of Trade should require all persons operating certain specified agreements to apply to the tribunal for a declaration that such agreements were not against the public interest. It would then fall upon any objectors to show that the agreements were against the public interest. The statement went on to outline several criteria which would help the tribunal to decide the issue. It also claimed that the Monopoly Commission's terms of reference should be re-defined so as to prevent overlapping and duplication. This reflected the feeling of many industrialists that the Monopolies Commission was unfair in that it acted as prosecutor, judge and jury. Therefore many of them were keen to have the power of the Commission reduced.

The only other important publication produced by the three peak associations was in 1956, and consisted of a joint statement of views. In February 1956, the leaders of the F.B.I., N.U.M. and A.B.C.C. met to discuss concerted action on the impending legislation, and agreed that as far as possible the three bodies should attempt to be in harmony. As a result, they agreed to form a joint committee to deal with the issues arising when the Bill was laid before Parliament. The joint statement which outlined their views on the Bill as introduced was published on 5 March 1956. It warmly welcomed the judicial approach which the government had finally decided to adopt, but expressed concern at the procedure whereby an agreement was assumed to be against the public interest unless it could pass one of the seven 'gateways' in the Bill. This was, it argued, akin to assuming that a man was guilty until he had proved his innocence. The joint statement objected to the principle that the burden of showing an agreement to be in the public interest was placed upon the parties to the agreement. It repeated the alarm felt by industry that, having passed one of the specified tests laid down in the Bill, the parties to the agreement still had to show that the agreement did not harm anyone else, *i.e.* they had to prove an *absence* of harm rather than the Registrar having to prove an *existence* of harm. In the view of industrialists 'it would be reasonable if the Crown were to have to prove an agreement to be harmful to others and the parties to the agreement allowed to answer the allegation of damage'. The statement also criticized the definition of classes of agreements to be registered, and in fact the Bill was later amended to meet some of the criticism on this point. With regard to R.P.M., the increased powers of individual enforcement were welcomed, though the statement argued for some kind of collective enforcement of R.P.M. [This attitude was also adopted by the retail organizations led by the Fair Prices Defence Committee and the P.A.T.A.] The joint statement as outlined above was sent to the President of the Board of Trade and M.P.s.

Publicity in the form of pamphlets and prepared statements is not the only form of publicity which trade associations managed to obtain. Informal statements, speeches and letters to the press all helped to publicize their case. For example, in February 1955, after press criticism of its private courts, the motor trade had sent representatives from all over the country to defend the price maintenance policy of the British Motor Traders' Association before the press. Also, the Secretary of the P.A.T.A. wrote to *The Times* on two occasions, defending the collective enforcement of R.P.M. and claiming that small firms would not have the resources to enforce their rights without it. Similarly, the Secretary of the British Motor Traders'

69

Association wrote to *The Times* claiming that individual enforcement of R.P.M. was too expensive for most firms. He seemed to recognize the public criticism of trade association courts and proposed therefore that they should be brought under the surveillance of the ordinary courts. The Deputy Chairman of Dunlop wrote to *The Times* expressing his concern that the issue of price maintenance was 'apparently being prejudged as much by those who guide public opinion as by the public at large'. The views of industry had also been given wide publicity when the Monopolies Commission Report was published, and again when the Bill received its First Reading.

Consultation and negotiation

Publicity is of course only one technique (and almost certainly the least effective) used to influence governments, and large scale publicity campaigns are usually the last resort of pressure groups. Their main method of influencing the government was by consultation and negotiation. The process of consultation had begun with the Monopolies Commission and was certainly intensified after publication of the Report. Many references are made in the annual reports of the peak associations, and of various trade associations, to frequent meetings between the Minister, his civil servants and representatives of industry. For example, when the Report was published the views of the F.B.I. were 'conveyed to the President of the Board of Trade' (*F.B.I. Annual Report*, 1955, 7). When Mr. Thorneycroft announced the broad lines of the government's policy in the debate on the Commission's Report, the Federation took part in further discussions with him. In September

1955 detailed representations were submitted to him which contained a number of proposals. These were largely concerned with the nature of the tribunal and the onus of justification which industries called before it would have to discharge. Like the rest of industry, the Federation again argued very strongly that the tribunal should be a judicial body, as it believed this to be the only way to ensure complete objectivity and impartiality. It strongly opposed the appointment of a lay tribunal to advise the Minister, and argued again in favour of the collective enforcement of R.P.M. where it was the most efficient method. The Federation discussed its views with the President again in November 1955, and according to its Annual Report for 1955 it had several other discussions with the President and his advisers in the autumn of that year on the subject of the proposed legislation. The F.P.D.C. also sent a deputation to the President in 1955, to press the case for the collective enforcement of R.P.M., and after its meeting with him it decided 'to keep in touch with officials of the Board with a view to consultations regarding the drafting of new legislation' (*F.P.D.C. Chairman's Report*, 1956, 5). The suggestions of the P.A.T.A. were conveyed to Mr. Thorneycroft by its secretary and were repeated in a formal statement on the subject of R.P.M. submitted by the F.P.D.C. in 1956. This statement strongly advocated that the tribunal should be a judicial body.

Early in 1956 reports of the contents of the proposed Bill had begun to circulate amongst trade associations and, in view of this, the P.A.T.A. made further representations to Mr. Thorneycroft expressing its concern. The P.A.T.A. *Quarterly Record* records that Mr. Thorneycroft stated that these and other representations had been taken into account in the drafting of the Bill (*Quarterly Record*, April

71

1955, 11). In January 1956, *The Financial Times* reported that the Bill had been considerably delayed, and that until it was actually published it was not clear whether or not Mr. Thorneycroft had been pushed beyond the limit in the concessions he had had to make. It was, the paper argued, 'clear that he has been pushed very close to it' (*The Financial Times*, 21 January 1956). In February *The Observer*, in similar vein, suggested that several earlier and much harsher drafts had been abandoned or drastically revised during the previous two months after reports of earlier drafts had been circulated.

As we have seen, industrialists were particularly concerned about the *type* of tribunal which was to be adopted. They considered that some kind of legislation was inevitable, and so made every attempt to ensure that whatever legislation was finally introduced should be as fair as possible and should, in addition, allow industry sufficient room to manœuvre. As a result, a judicial tribunal was the only type of tribunal likely to satisfy industry. The Bill did in fact set up a judicial court in response to these pressures and industrialists warmly welcomed this. The N.U.M., in its annual report for 1955/6, commented that the Bill 'showed that the main point of the National Union's case had been conceded: the special court to be set up was a judicial one' (p. 25).

After the publication of the Bill, the joint committee of the three peak associations sent a deputation to Thorneycroft to put their agreed views to him. They also formed a drafting committee which eventually drafted over sixty amendments to the Bill. According to the A.B.C.C. 'every possible attempt was made to secure support for them from the government' (*Annual Report*, 1956). The F.B.I., through the joint committee, also maintained

72

close contact with the Board of Trade throughout the passage of the Bill.

The most effective pressure undoubtedly took place before the Bill was introduced, although it did not cease after its introduction. Where no concessions could be gained either from Thorneycroft or the Board of Trade, the organized interests concentrated their efforts on M.P.s. For example, the P.A.T.A. sent a circular to its members asking all of them to contact their M.P.s in order to familiarize them both with the P.A.T.A.s arguments and with the likely content and function of amendments which the Association was going to draft. A number of M.P.s did eventually propose amendments drafted by the Association. The A.B.C.C. also asked its members to seek support from their local M.P.s for the amendments drafted by the joint committee. The committee was in close contact with interested M.P.s and Peers throughout the passage of the Bill, and in February 1956 a well-attended meeting of the Conservative Trade and Industry Committee met representatives of the peak associations to hear a summary of their views.

The joint drafting committee was particularly helped in this respect by the fact that at least eight Conservative M.P.s were at that time office-holders in one or other of the organizations (one M.P. was a member of the drafting committee). A number of Conservative M.P.s also had connections with various other trade associations likely to be affected by the legislation. These institutional ties of course helped industry considerably, as Conservative M.P.s could lobby inside their own party at backbench meetings. (It was even rumoured that there had been an attempt by some backbenchers to get Thorneycroft removed from the Board of Trade.) Thus industry had little difficulty in

73

finding M.P.s who were prepared both to argue their case in debate and to move amendments in committee stage. Evidence of the satisfaction felt by industry on this score is provided in the F.B.I. Annual Report for 1956, which records that 'industry's views, though by no means always accepted, were . . . thoroughly voiced during the many debates on the issue' (p. 5). The Conservative M.P.s who had close contacts with trade associations received a certain amount of criticism from *The Economist* which, labelling them the trade association Tories, considered them to be the 'villains of the piece, who have put down a shoal of amendments, including at least a score that could destroy the whole effectiveness of the Bill' (*The Economist*, 21 April 1956). This was a somewhat emotional view, as it could be argued that the M.P.s concerned were performing a useful constitutional role, i.e. representing the views of outside interests in Parliament, just as the organized interests were performing the legitimate and useful function of attempting to influence the government's policy. In fact the peak association drafting committee drafted many of the amendments for the M.P.s and provided them with detailed briefs explaining the amendments. Although most of the industrial amendments emanated from this committee, some trade associations acted independently. For example, the S.M.M.T. proposed four amendments in connection with R.P.M. and provided briefs for the M.P.s moving these amendments. A considerable number of industrial amendments were accepted by the government—so many in fact that the F.B.I. could with considerable satisfaction record in its Annual Report that 'few Bills have suffered so many changes in detail during the Parliamentary stages'. However, as will be explained in Chapter 7, by no means all of them were accepted.

The debate on the Monopolies Commission Report

On 13 July 1955, the House of Commons had debated the
Monopolies Commission Report, the debate being based on
a government motion welcoming the Report as a basis
on which proposals could be formulated. The vague and
non-committal wording of the motion however reflected
the government's indecision at the time. The government
was taking a very cautious approach to the problem and
regarded this debate as somewhat exploratory. The political correspondent of *The Observer*, suggesting that the
wording of the motion had only been decided the day
before the debate, claimed that it was the result of an
almost fifty-fifty division of Conservative members on the
issue (*The Observer*, 17 July 1955).

The debate gave the first public indication of the government's attitude. Basically, the government had decided
that registration of agreements, followed by individual examination and judgement, was the most suitable procedure. But they also felt that the onus of showing agreements to be in the public interest should be placed 'fairly
and squarely on the shoulders of the men who use them'
(*Hansard*, 13 July 1955, Col. 1944). Mr. Thorneycroft was
particularly vague on the form that the tribunal should
take. He thought that on the one hand there were power-
ful arguments in favour of having a judge, and on the other
of having a Minister responsible for the final decision. He
considered that this was a question upon which the views
of the House of Commons would be extremely valuable.
The explanation of the Government's hesitation is fairly

75

clear, as there were widespread reports that the Cabinet itself was split on the issue but that Thorneycroft had persuaded the P.M. to give his backing to a Bill. Division certainly existed amongst Conservative backbenchers. As we have seen, a number of them had connections with trade associations so that any legislation directed against such associations was bound to cause controversy within the party. On the other hand, public opinion, or most people's estimation of it, demanded some kind of action. *The Observer* commented that because of the division within the party anything or almost nothing might happen over the next twelve months (17 July 1955). But this interpretation of the situation was not correct. To take action certainly did risk a split within the party, but to take no action at all would have been just as politically dangerous. The Labour Party would without doubt have made a great deal of political capital out of the issue if the Conservatives had given in to vested interests. Also, just as there were Conservative backbenchers who were against taking action, there were other backbenchers who felt that the party should deal with restrictive practices (for example, the twelve backbenchers who had written 'Change is Our Ally'). To have taken no action would have therefore created just as much division within the party. As it was, soon after the 1959 election, the leadership of the Conservative Trade and Industry Committee was changed, thus removing a number of trade association M.P.s. This seemed to reflect a degree of impatience which some backbenchers felt with regard to some of their more restrictionist colleagues. The evidence also suggests that Mr. Thorneycroft himself wished to take action against restrictionism. As Dr. Mc. I. Johnson has since argued, 'The President of the Board of Trade was determined to get his Bill' and was 'in

76

no mood for grace and favour' (Johnson, 1958, 79 and 81).

The government's indecision clearly encouraged intensive lobbying between the debate in July 1955 and the introduction of the Bill. This was particularly true of the type of tribunal to be adopted, even though it was believed that Thorneycroft personally favoured a tribunal responsible to a Minister. The intervening period saw some fairly bitter controversy within the party and it appears that there were a number of stormy backbench meetings about the issue. (*The Economist*, for example, reported that Mr. Thorneycroft was having a fearful tussle behind the scenes.) The division within the party helped the organized interests considerably as it helped to introduce a degree of flexibility into the process. When the Bill was finally introduced, *The Financial Times* accurately described it as not exactly the Bill Thorneycroft would have wanted but what he had been able to persuade the Cabinet to accept (16 February 1956).

A compromise Bill

The resultant Bill was therefore a compromise which emerged from the complex system of conflict which had surrounded the issue all along. Total prohibition of restrictive practices had been rejected, and individual case by case examination had been adopted. However, collective enforcement of R.P.M. had been banned despite the Minority Commission Report. Also, again contrary to the Minority Report, the terms under which each case was to be considered had been fairly clearly defined. The Bill, nevertheless, contained many proposals in line with the representation which had been made. The F.B.I. welcomed the case by case approach compared with the Majority

Commission proposals which it had earlier considered to be totally unacceptable. The most significant proposal as regards conforming with the views of industry was the decision to set up a court. That the government had great difficulty in making the issue justiciable was very clear. The Lord Chancellor (Lord Kilmuir) revealed in a speech in March 1956 that he and his colleagues had spent 'many anxious weeks trying to work out a truly justiciable issue'. Later, in his memoirs, he records that all the legal talent at the government's disposal exerted its ingenuity to find true questions of fact which the court could properly decide (Kilmuir, 1964, 262). This caused a certain amount of anxiety in the judiciary and Kilmuir met a number of judges in order to reassure them that 'they would be doing their own work and not expressing political views' (Kilmuir, 1964, 262).

The passage of the Bill and the ensuing attempts to amend it still further will be described in the next chapter.

7

The passage of the Bill through Parliament

The Second Reading debate was, of course, the first occasion on which the Bill was discussed in Parliament. The division inside the House fell into three fairly well-defined units. The first unit may be described as the President of the Board of Trade plus his backbench supporters (i.e. those broadly in favour of a stronger and more effective Bill). The second unit was the official Opposition, which was also in favour of a strong and effective Bill. Although divisions did exist within the Parliamentary Labour party, these were not very significant in 1956 and indeed were not all that evident. The third unit was what *The Economist* called the trade association Tories. This was the group of backbenchers in the Conservative ranks which was basically opposed to the Bill and anxious to amend it in favour of the industrial interests.

The President outlined the main provisions of the Bill and put forward his justifications for the proposals. His position seemed to be that of a minister defending a policy, some details of which he disagreed with, in the sense that

79

he would probably have preferred a stronger measure. He pointed out that conditions had changed since the 1930s when many of the practices had arisen. His view was that although the agreements might be beneficial, they had certain defects which the country could ill afford in an age of technical change. Because the agreements had both good and bad effects, it was necessary for someone to judge whether or not the practices were against the public interest, and the people least qualified to do this were those who operated the practices.

He dealt at length with the machinery for judging the practices, and argued against having a government department responsible for enforcing the legislation. In his opinion, it would not be in the national interest to have the Board of Trade and a given industry as rival contestants on an issue. His intention was to remove the issues from the political to the judicial sphere because an administrative solution would mean that a government minister would have to study a very long report on each case, and would then have to defend it in the House of Commons. This would involve the House in very detailed discussions about particular restrictive schemes. However, he did concede that the decisions were not only decisions of fact and law, but also involved economic and social judgements. He claimed that he had always been unashamedly and wholeheartedly in favour of the judicial solution, which he recognized as being a new and perhaps adventurous constitutional advance. Nevertheless he felt that the judiciary was well able to adapt itself to change. This contrasts sharply with his earlier statement in 1955, in the debate on the Monopolies Commission Report on Collective Discrimination, when he seemed undecided on this very issue.

During the Second Reading debate, the Minister made

particular reference to the tailpiece of the controversial clause specifying criteria for deciding the public interest. He stressed that an industry, having passed one of the specified tests or gateways, must *further* show that the restriction had not operated to an unreasonable extent to the detriment of other persons or otherwise to the detriment of the public interest. This tailpiece was eventually amended by the Government after considerable pressure from industry (described in previous chapter). He also emphasized that price rings and level tendering had been included in the Bill, even though these had not been investigated by the Commission. It should be remembered that this aspect of restrictionism had received considerable adverse publicity in 1955. The Minister defended the reduction in the size of the Monopolies Commission, by explaining that the government was anxious to prevent any overlap between the Commission and the Restrictive Practices Court. We have already noted in connection with this, that certain sections of industry had severely criticized the Commission over the years as being prosecutor, judge and jury rolled into one. Many years later, in 1964, *The Economist* suggested that this section of the 1956 Act was part of a quid pro quo for industry's acceptance of the Bill as a whole. It is of course impossible to prove that the reduction in size of the Commission was a direct result of pressure from industry, although support is lent to this view by the fact that the Conservative government in a White Paper in 1964 proposed that the size of the Commission should be increased again.

In dealing with the Bill's proposals concerning R.P.M., the President commented that this was the first, though probably not the last legislative proposal in this field. In fact in 1964, Mr. Heath managed to force through a measure virtually banning all R.P.M. The 1956 Bill completely banned all *collective* enforcement of R.P.M. The Minister argued that it would be very unwise to set up a body to examine each case of collective enforcement of R.P.M. since in his view, such a procedure would be unworkable and would last for an eternity. This was exactly the argument used by the official Opposition against the government's proposals for dealing with other cases of restrictionism.

Mr. Jay, for the Opposition, moved an amendment asking the House not to give the Bill a Second Reading, because in the Opposition's view, it failed to provide speedy and effective action to protect the public. He said that the procedure laid down in the Bill would be extremely slow, and he predicted that the first case would not be decided within two years and that the first class of agreements would not be cleared within five years. The Opposition strongly advocated that the proposals of the Majority Report of the Commission be adopted, because under these, the time needed for each case would be much less, as some procedure for *prima facie* exemptions could be devised. Mr. Jay attacked the proposal to set up a court of law, and argued that the vital decisions to be taken in this field were questions of public interest and not questions of law or fact. The Opposition felt that such decisions should be taken by a minister responsible to Parliament. The situation was, he suggested, akin to handing over the Budget to a court of law and asking it to take all steps necessary for the prosperity of the country! The Opposition was also very much against the proposal to reduce the size of the Commission. They criticized the Bill's proposals dealing with R.P.M. although they supported the abolition of its collective enforcement. Thus they had

82

modified their stand of 1951. Mr. Jay now argued that there should be some public authority to protect the public, either by price control or by some other method. In 1951 the Labour government had declared its intention of *abolishing* individual enforcement of R.P.M., whereas in 1956 the party thought that the Bill's proposals strengthing individual R.P.M. went too far, and that as a result some *safeguards* were necessary.

The third unit in the House, those Conservatives anxious to weaken the Bill, had little opportunity to speak during the Second Reading. However, Sir Lancelot Joynson-Hicks did voice one or two of the criticisms that had been made by industry, and which were to be the basis of amendments proposed during the Committee stage. He welcomed the Bill on the grounds that both the public and industrialists had a feeling of security when they were in the hands of the judiciary. He felt that the feeling would not be present if the decisions on this issue were left in the hands of the politicians. But his complaint against the Bill was that Part I placed too much emphasis on the Registrar. He thought that the Registrar should be appointed by the Lord Chancellor, and that his duty should be to ensure that full information was laid before the Court from every angle. The Court would then be able to arrive at a fair, proper and impartial decision. Sir Lancelot also complained, as did an earlier backbencher, that the tailpiece referred to by the Minister was unfair since the parties to the agreement had to prove a negative. As we have seen in the previous chapter, this was one of the main criticisms voiced by the industrial interests, and was the subject of many of the amendments proposed by the F.B.I./N.U.M./A.B.C.C. Committee. However, it became clear during the Second Reading, that the

83

Minister could rely on the votes of the Opposition if necessary to defeat any of the wrecking amendments proposed by those backbenchers opposed to the Bill.

THE COMMITTEE AND REPORT STAGES : OPEN CONFLICT

Group activity during the Committee and Report Stages of Bills, has become accepted as part of the normal process by which a Bill becomes law (Stewart, 1958). When an interest group attempts to amend a Bill during its passage through Parliament, this is not regarded as breaking any unwritten rules of the game, and in no way harms the relationship between the groups and the government. In fact, interest groups often discuss proposed amendments with ministers and civil servants before tabling them in Parliament. In this sense the Committee and Report stages are not so much a struggle, but more a process of wary collaboration conducted according to accepted behavioural norms. For example, it was reported that the President of the Board of Trade had approached various trade associations during the passage of the Bill, in order to persuade them to advise their M.P.s to either withdraw or modify certain proposed amendments. It has been suggested that the most important aspect of the amending process as far as interest groups are concerned, is that the government has to make a public and reasoned decision on various issues. Interest groups can, however, gain far more than this. Often a group can succeed in amending a Bill so that life under the new legislation is made easier from their point of view. At the same time, the Bill is improved as far as the government and civil servants are concerned. In addition to changes in detail, interest groups may also attempt to change a Bill more drastically. Thus in 1956,

84

several amendments were put down by backbenchers on behalf of the various interests, which, if accepted, would have wrecked the main provisions of the Bill.

The remainder of this section deals with the attempts that were made to resolve the various issues of conflict as the Bill passed through its Committee and Report stages.

The onus of proof

The main issue between the government and the opponents of the Bill was that of the onus of proof under the terms of the Bill. The Minister had firmly stated his belief that the onus of proof before the Court should be placed firmly on the shoulders of those operating the agreements, whereas opponents of the Bill argued that the question of the public interest should be left more open for the Court to decide either way. Sir Lionel Heald, a former Attorney-General and one of the leading opponents of the Bill, moved an amendment which would have shifted the onus of proof. This amendment specified that the preparation and presentation of any proceedings by the Registrar, should be conducted in such a way as to ensure that all relevant facts and circumstances would be placed before the Court, whether these were in favour or against the interests of the parties to the agreement. In his view, this would ensure that the proceedings before the Court would be fair, square and above board. The amendment was supported by many other Conservative backbenchers connected with industry, and was of course very much in line with the views of the peak associations. The Minister refused to accept the amendment on the grounds that it would blur one of the essentials of the Bill. He pointed out that the onus of proof was a concomitant to the judicial approach. In other words, the Minister appeared to be saying that if industry wanted a Court which was itself an important concession, then it must accept the burden of proof as part of the bargain. Without it the Bill would be so weak as to be useless. In the face of this Ministerial opposition, the amendment was withdrawn.

The court

Sir L. Ungoed-Thomas, one of the main Opposition spokesmen, moved an amendment which if it had been carried, would have set up a tribunal rather than a Court. It proposed a tribunal of fourteen members responsible to a Minister, and reflected the Opposition's view that the issues were economic and political, and not justiciable. The Minister replied that the Courts were not unused to deciding such issues (although as Lord Kilmuir later revealed, the judges were not over-anxious to take on this new task), and he was supported by several of his own backbenchers. One leading backbencher connected with a trade association declared that he was very glad to be able to support the Minister on this issue, as he did not feel that he would be able to support him on much else in the Bill. In his view, the Restrictive Practices Court would command much more respect than a body like the Monopolies Commission. Concerning the *composition* of the Court, another Conservative backbencher moved an amendment to the effect that the proposed lay members of the court should have *experience* of industry, commerce and public affairs, rather than *knowledge* and experience in these fields. This reflected the fears of traders and manufacturers who felt that they would be lectured from on high when they

86

appeared before the Court. The amendment was supported by other backbenchers connected with trade associations, but was withdrawn when the Minister pointed out that this would greatly narrow the choice of persons available. The Labour party by contrast, proposed an amendment which would have enabled greater consumer representation among the lay members of the court. This amendment was also rejected by the government.

Agreements to be registered

The clause dealing with the types of agreements which were to be registered provides an example of the type of detailed concessions which interest groups commonly gain during the passage of a Bill. Thus Captain L. P. S. Orr (Conservative) moved an amendment to exempt from registration, those payments made to a trade association which were concerned solely with industrial and scientific research or with the administrative expenses of the association. This was accepted by the Parliamentary Secretary to the Board of Trade, and in no way weakened the Bill. There were in fact a great many detailed amendments of this kind which though not important in terms of public policy, were nonetheless of importance to the interest groups whose operations would otherwise have been unnecessarily inconvenienced.

Judicial investigation of registered agreements

Under this section of the Bill, the Labour Party introduced an important amendment designed to ban, within eighteen months of the passing of the Act, all collective agreements considered in the Monopolies Commission Report. Mr. Jay claimed that their intention was identical

87

to that of the government with regard to collective enforcement of R.P.M. He argued that the practices condemned by the Commission Report should be declared unlawful in the same way that the government had declared collective enforcement of R.P.M. unlawful. In his view, the issue was whether or not the residue of hardship which might possibly fall on some producers and traders if the practices were banned, outweighed the hardships suffered by consumers if the agreements continued. In rejecting the amendment, the Minister replied that the two systems were similar, unless the Opposition wanted all agreements to be banned after eighteen months whether or not they had been examined by the Court. He also thought that the Opposition amendment would only prohibit the enforcement procedures, and would not strike at the root of the trouble, i.e. the practices themselves. Mr. Jay countered that if this were so, then why had the government referred collective enforcement to the Commission in the first place? Mr. Holt for the Liberals suggested that it was the publicity that was given to trade association courts, which induced the public mind to support this sort of legislation. Mr. Thorneycroft with commendable frankness, admitted that on this point he was somewhat vulnerable, but explained that at the time of the first general reference, they had had little experience of common-price agreements and level tendering. He said that either way, whether he had been right or wrong in 1952, he intended to be right now. During the discussion of this clause, R. Harris (Conservative) strongly defended the private court system used by trade associations, and moved an amendment which if it had been accepted would have allowed an association to enforce by civil proceedings, an agreement found not to be against the public interest by the Restrictive Practices

88

Court, but the government refused to accept this amendment, and it was withdrawn.

Definition of the public interest

The clause defining the criteria which the Court should apply in deciding the public interest, caused the most controversy in the House. The Labour party made several attempts to restrict the number of gateways that industries could plead—for example, they moved an amendment to remove safety of the public as justification for an agreement. Their argument, like that of the Majority Commission Report, was that if safety of the public were involved, then special legislation should be introduced to cover this. Conservative backbenchers who were opposed to the Bill tried to amend the clause in the opposite direction, i.e. they wanted to widen the scope for exemptions which industries would be allowed to plead. To take one instance of this, Sir Peter Roberts moved an amendment to permit an industry to claim, in defence of an agreement, that it prevented temporary unemployment. Similarly, Sir J. Hutchison (Conservative) put down an amendment to allow industry to plead that banning an agreement might have an adverse effect on the availability of skilled labour. Neither of these amendments was accepted by the government. A sub-section of the clause in question already allowed as justification of an agreement, that it prevented serious and persistent unemployment. Angus Maude, another Conservative backbencher, argued against his fellow backbenchers and suggested that the sub-section as it stood *originally* was an impediment to economic progress, and that far from being widened, it should be withdrawn. W. Shepherd (Conservative) also suggested that the sub-section

89

was too large a loophole and should be taken out. It is interesting to note that this was one of the few occasions when Conservative backbenchers spoke in favour of strengthening the Bill, although it did serve to show that the Minister was not completely without support from his own side.

The Conservative M.P.s opposed to the Bill were, however, successful in obtaining an amendment to the tailpiece of this section of the Bill, as noted in the previous chapter. In response to pressure, the Minister introduced an amendment to give the Court the duty of *balancing* any advantage which had been shown under the gateways, against any detriment to the public. This met the very strong representations that industry made, claiming that they had to prove an absence of harm, and it was therefore claimed by the three peak associations as one of their major successes during the passage of the Bill. The Labour party opposed the amendment as being a totally unnecessary concession to industry, and moreover, they felt that it had been introduced solely as a result of representations made since the Second Reading. Mr. Fletcher for the Opposition said that he understood that the sting was always in the tailpiece, but that now the government was taking the sting out therefore rendering it almost nugatory. Mr. Thorneycroft replied that it had been felt in some quarters, that having passed through one or more of the gateways, the issue was going to be started anew without any relation to what had already been established in passing one or more of the gateways. The amendment was warmly welcomed by a number of Conservative backbenchers. However, R. Harris (Conservative) remained critical about the whole clause because he disliked 'a system under which people go before a division of the High Court and are guilty before they open their mouths'. It was his view that the onus of proof should be on the Registrar anyway, and as a result he would only support the Minister in the Lobby with 'dragging feet'.

Enforcement of R.P.M.

The clause dealing with R.P.M. also aroused considerable controversy. Sir Hugh Linstead (Conservative) expressed the view that the Minister was hardening his mind increasingly against making it at all possible for any reasonable form of R.P.M. to be operated. A number of Conservative backbenchers argued strongly for the retention of collective enforcement of R.P.M., and put down an amendment designed to allow a trade association to take action on behalf of an individual trader. However, Angus Maude again tried to correct the impression that all Conservative backbenchers were against the Minister. He argued that there was a considerable majority of his Honourable Friends who entirely agreed with the solution that the government had adopted. On the Labour side, a determined effort was mounted to secure exemption from the R.P.M. clause for the Co-operatives, but this move was defeated.

The Monopolies Commission

Many Labour members supported amendments intended to keep the Commission the same size, as they felt that it was wrong to assume that the work of the Commission would be reduced as a result of the Bill. These amendments were defeated. At this stage, Sir Lionel Heald voiced some of industry's criticisms of the Commission, and asked the Minister if he would examine its procedure.

The Committee and Report stages of the passage of

91

the Bill were characterized by the collapse of the predicted Conservative revolt. No Conservative M.P. voted against the Government or even abstained. Even M.P.s bitterly opposed to the Bill went into the division lobbies in support of the government. The wrecking amendments proposed by these backbenchers were always withdrawn and not pressed to a division. An important inhibiting factor in this respect was of course the attitude of the official Opposition, who proposed many strengthening and tougher amendments. Quite simply, any wrecking amendments had little chance of success when the Minister had refused them. Once the Bill had been introduced, the Minister seemed determined with few exceptions, not to have the Bill seriously weakened. However, the opponents of the Bill did manage to secure a number of concessions from him, varying in importance.

THE THIRD READING

The Minister reaffirmed his belief that the government had successfully adapted the judicial system to meet present-day economic needs. He considered that they had managed to substitute the impartial and informed judgement of a Court in place of the day-to-day cut and thrust of Parliamentary dispute. The procedure finally adopted would be both fair and efficient, and the public generally would be glad to see the end of collective enforcement of R.P.M. 'with the massive and complicated arrangements for private courts'.

Sir L. Ungoed-Thomas for the Opposition, reiterated their belief that the system of prohibition, as applied to collective enforcement of R.P.M., should have been further extended. They were very much in favour of a scheme of prohibition coupled with examination of a narrow range of exceptions. In the Opposition's view, the Bill was a muddled proposal which tried to wed what was basically an economic decision, with what was essentially a justiciable process.

Sir Lionel Heald (Conservative) argued that the Press suggestion that he was a leading rebel trying to wreck the whole Bill, had been disproved by events. However, in his view, the Conservative party was undertaking something that amounted to a serious interference with private enterprise and private industry. Despite this overall view, he thought that they had improved the Bill considerably, and thanked the Minister for paying attention to the trade associations and professional bodies. Referring specifically to the amendment to the tailpiece of the public interest clause, he commented that they had obtained a provision which would no doubt be difficult to work, but which would deal with the matter in a fair way. R. Harris (Conservative) likened the Minister to the piano often depicted in cartoons and jokes: he had been pushed in opposite directions from both ends but had remained standing in the middle. However, he hoped that the new Court would enjoy the confidence of trade and industry to a greater extent than the Monopolies Commission had done.

The passage of the Bill in the Lords proved to be very similar to its passage through the Commons. Conservative Peers put down amendments supported by, and favourable to, trade associations. They withdrew them after assurances from the government, or because there was no hope of getting them carried. Similarly Opposition Peers proposed amendments, but they were defeated in division, as they had been in the Commons.

THE PASSAGE OF THE BILL: AN OVERALL VIEW

The Bill received the Royal assent on 2 August 1956. In *The Observer*'s view it had emerged remarkably unscathed. This view was shared by most commentators at the time. The predicted revolt by Conservative backbenchers had not materialized. Certain of the backbenchers had clearly been subject to cross-pressures arising from conflicting roles, but these were not sufficient to break party discipline. There were probably five main factors preventing a revolt within the Conservative party:

1 The official Opposition: *The Financial Times* for example, considered that pressure from the Labour Opposition had been Mr. Thorneycroft's strongest weapon. (Similarly R. Butt has suggested that Mr. Heath was helped in his dealings with his own party, by the fact that the Labour party, though divided, contained a number of R.P.M. abolitionists in 1964.) (Butt, 1967, 270.)
2 As a counterbalance to Conservative opponents of the Bill, there was an equally strong, though not vociferous, body of Conservative backbenchers pressing the Minister to stand firm.
3 Public opinion, as it was reported and stimulated by the Press.
4 The Monopolies Commission Report helped to reinforce these first three factors.
5 Mr Thorneycroft's personal role in standing firm.

8

The policy process

The preceding chapters have been concerned with the background, passage and content of the Restrictive Trade Practices Act. We must now assess the significance of this study as an analysis of the policy-making process in Britain. The most essential point to be borne in mind in attempting to draw conclusions about the policy process in a study of this kind, is that it involves a particular set of factors interacting in particular circumstances at a particular point in time. In this way, each example of the policy-making process is unique, and therefore, it is impossible to make firm generalizations on the basis of one case study. In addition, almost any case study is going to be based on essentially limited information about events and the behaviour of participants.

However, while such a study may not justify broad generalizations about the process, it may raise interesting questions about the workings of the process and the role of interest groups within it. This chapter attempts to examine the main questions which emerge from the study. These can be grouped under three headings. Firstly, the economic and moral constraints which bounded the process will be discussed. Secondly, we can analyse the area of manœuvrability within this constricting framework, and the role of interest groups. Finally, because the workings of these processes take place within a framework of institutions, the relevance of this study to the functioning of these institutions in terms of public policy, will be suggested.

ECONOMIC AND MORAL CONSTRAINTS

The Restrictive Trade Practices Act dealt with an economic problem which set certain limits on possible legislative action. The economic environment imposed certain constraints upon political action. Purely economic factors were an incentive to government action because of the need to increase the efficiency of the British economy. Despite this economic need, however, the government was faced with the problem of availability of information. In this sense, information or at least the lack of it, acted as a further constraint within the political system. Initially, little was known about restrictive practices in Britain and because of this, the Monopolies Commission Report was particularly important as being the only authoritative account of the effects of the practices. This was all the more so since it was published at a time when the popular press was giving a great deal of adverse publicity to trade association activities. Thus the Monopolies Commission Report on Collective Discrimination is an example of a Commission of Inquiry which did not act as an instrument to avoid government action. On the contrary it made government action even more inevitable and unavoidable. But even though the Report provided the only concrete evidence on the problem, it was in many ways vulnerable

96

itself on this score, and this was in fact the basis of the Minority Report. The results of the decisions were consequently difficult to predict, particularly as the operation of the Act was removed from the control of government and Parliament. The whole question of amount of information available to policy makers is crucial to the efficiency of the policy-making process. It is not surprising that decisions are sometimes proved to be wrong at some future date, when it is realized that policy makers may of necessity have to take decisions based on conflicting or inadequate information. This information factor is likely to increase in importance as governments increase their degree of control and influence over the detailed workings of the economy.

The other overall constraint of importance in this case was a moral one. In any society there is a concept of justice, forming part of the political culture, which the government does not normally contravene. An example of such a concept is that a man is innocent until he is proved guilty. The Bill was criticized by the industrial interests as a breach of this fundamental principle because it contained the presumption that certain practices were against the public interest, unless they could pass one or more of the gateways. Because of all this it would probably have been politically impossible for the government to ban all restrictive trading agreements completely. Although the majority of observers considered that on the whole restrictive practices were bad, few were prepared to take the step of banning all agreements, because they considered it unjust to risk banning any innocent agreements that might exist. (The majority of the Commission of course claimed that they could not find any of these.) Similarly it was considered by the government that it

97

would be unjust to condemn agreements merely on the pleadings of the parties before a Court without having a full investigation. In this way it can be seen that rules of justice or rules of the game (Truman, 1951, 512) sometimes act as a check on the policy process. On the other hand, however, the concept of justice provided one of the motivating forces for legislation, because it was believed that public opinion was hostile towards private trade association courts, and considered them to be unjust. The T.U.C. for example, seemed to find these courts the main objection to the restrictive practices in question.

THE AREA OF MANŒUVRABILITY AND THE ROLE OF THE ORGANIZED INTERESTS

Clearly the organized interests in this case were playing a defensive role. The Bill was directed at the practices operated by many trade associations, and it therefore fell upon them to defend their position in order to maintain the status quo. This defensive role did not prevent the interests from gaining important concessions. As R. Rose suggests, a group must be prepared to modify its tactics when its demands 'appear to be inconsistent with the predominant cultural norms' (Rose, 1965, 129). We can see an example of this flexibility in the attitude of the F.B.I. which, at the time, took the view that industry should accept action along the lines of the Minority Commission Report. In this way the interests did not isolate themselves by adopting uncompromising opposition to government policy, but instead concentrated on an efficient and reasoned presentation of their case. The secret of their success seems to be that, as Professor Finer argues, most of the lobbying was done silently and not in the glare of publicity (Finer, 1966, 59). The groups did not make the mistake of publicly forcing the government into intransigence.

The area of manœuvrability within which the interest groups were able to operate was increased by three factors. Firstly, they were greatly helped by the ignorance of the public about the true significance of the practices. The setting up of a court of law to deal with restrictionism was, for example, unlikely to cause adverse reaction. The main point as far as the public was concerned was that private courts were being abolished, and common price agreements and level tendering were being dealt with. The government had taken action to deal with the problem and that was that. In such a situation, important concessions were possible as they were unlikely to cause any public outcry. Secondly, the governing party was divided so that the organized interests had access to a block of M.P.s on the government benches who were prepared to move and support amendments, and who were prepared to argue for the groups in party meetings. The position of the groups would undoubtedly have been weaker had the party been completely united against restrictive practices. Thirdly, the fact that the Commission Report was also divided, almost certainly helped the groups, because it allowed some room for doubt about the effects of the practices under investigation.

However, as suggested in the previous chapter, the area of manœuvrability was reduced by several factors. Firstly, the Majority of the Commission had condemned the practices as being against the public interest, and this was continually quoted by those anxious for an attack on restrictionism. We have noted earlier that at least one Conservative M.P. expressed the view that whatever was in the Report would eventually reach the Statute Book, and this meant that the Report set certain limits on possible concessions to group influence. Secondly, the Minister in charge of the Bill acted as a rock against which much of the group backbench pressure foundered. Had a weaker Minister been in charge of the Board of Trade, it is likely that the Bill would have either not been introduced or would have been weakened beyond recognition. Thus the importance of the individual in the policy process must be stressed. A similar example of this importance of the personality of the individual office-holder, can be seen in the case of Edward Heath at the Board of Trade, with his determination to abolish R.P.M. despite group and party pressure (Butt, R., 1967, chapter 9). Also Self and Storing (1962, 126) have stated that part of the reason for the abolition of agricultural committees after the Franks Report, despite N.F.U. opposition, was the Minister's 'unusually independent attitude towards the N.F.U'. Thirdly, the Minister was helped in his stand by those backbenchers within his own party, who believed that an attack on restrictionism was desirable as part of a policy of free enterprise, and who in doing so managed to show that the Conservative Party was more than a set of sectional interests. A fourth restraint, reinforcing the others, was the amount of adverse press and public criticism accorded to the activities of trade associations in 1955/6. This would certainly have strengthened the hand of the Minister against those of his Cabinet colleagues who opposed action against trade associations and to this extent we can consider public opinion as an important factor in the policy-making process. Thus some policy decisions are taken with reference to supposed popular demand at a given time, and this may goad governments into action, although as we have seen in this case the actual form of action was not affected. The Board of Trade and other government departments may be considered as the fifth restraint on group influence, in that the evidence suggests that civil servants were in favour of some form of control over restrictive agreements. But the effectiveness of this check may have been reduced by the tradition of day-to-day co-operation between civil servant and interest group, which is one of the main characteristics of the British political system. This often desirable co-operative relationship seems to have placed the Board in a state of role-conflict which in turn influenced the working of the process. Finally, the Official Opposition acted as a sixth check on group influence, particularly during the passage of the Bill through Parliament. Having made political capital out of the government's alleged inactivity against restrictionism, the Opposition, despite its own internal divisions, played an important part in preventing a Conservative backbench revolt. Thus even though the Conservatives were divided, the government's own critics did not carry their dissent into the division lobby, as the Labour Opposition always supported Mr. Thorneycroft against any attempt to weaken the Bill. This suggests that on occasions when the governing party is divided and if this division is being exacerbated by outside interest, then the Opposition may be influential, however unwittingly, both in reinforcing party discipline in the governing party, and in defeating organized interests. Similarly R. Butt has argued that the attitude of the Labour party during the passage of the R.P.M. Bill in 1964 was an asset for Mr. Heath in his battle against his backbench rebels.

It would however be wrong to consider the organized interest groups as a completely adverse influence in the policy-making process. (The term *pressure* group has no doubt encouraged such inferences.) Interest groups provide a great deal of the information on which policy decisions are made. We have already commented on the problems which governments face when taking complex decisions on inadequate information. Without the information provided by groups, decisions would be even more likely to prove disastrous. Thus as Tivey and Wohlgemuth have suggested, 'no-one supposes that politicians and civil servants by themselves are capable of working out the effects of their actions except in general terms—and even then they are often wrong' (*Political Quarterly*, xxix, 1958, 70). Even the Monopolies Commission Report could not have been produced without the information provided by the interest groups, for the Report relied mainly on the groups for evidence about the working and effect of the practices. Also, as a result of the consultation which took place between the government and the groups, the Act emerged as an administratively tidier measure than when first introduced. It has been argued (McKenzie, R. T., *Political Quarterly*, xxix, 1958, 9-10) that interest groups may well provide a more efficient transmission belt for opinion than political parties. In 1955/6 the organized interests were certainly very efficient at transmitting both information and opinions to government, parliament and the civil service.

With regard to this role, the importance of the three peak associations must be stressed. The joint committee of the F.B.I./N.U.M./A.B.C.C. had the function of co-ordinating and processing the various views of the different trade associations involved, and of translating these into something approaching a uniform policy. In many ways, the peak associations acted like political parties in that they unified divergent opinions and interests, and in so doing performed an essential function within the political system. In the same way, the various bodies concerned with transport policy in Britain joined together to form the Central Co-ordinating Committee on Transport, in order to put their joint views to the Government during the passage of the 1968 Transport Bill. In general, the consultative process is likely to be more efficient if the government can deal with a single representative body, either for a particular industry or even for industry as a whole. Similarly, from the point of view of the groups themselves, their influence is likely to be greater if they combine forces in a united front, so avoiding any form of open group conflict. Such bodies may however find this task difficult at times. In 1955/6 for example, the F.B.I. did not find its representative role an easy one because its members were by no means united in their reaction to the government's proposals. Difficulties of this nature are of course likely to increase now that the F.B.I. and N.U.M. have merged with the British Employers Confederation, with the result that such bodies will themselves become more and more like the political system in which they operate.

IMPLICATIONS FOR PUBLIC POLICY

In his study of the passage of the 1946 Employment Act in the United States, S. K. Bailey suggested that a whole complex of factors combined and interacted to form the policy process (Bailey, 1950, 236). The evidence of the British case study which has been considered in this book, seems to confirm this interdependence of the political system. Bailey further argues that the various factors in the policy process acted only within the most generalized limits of popular concern about specific issues (*ibid.*). Again, similar conclusions can be drawn from the present study. As we have argued, public concern as stimulated by the press was an important motivational factor in the process, because participants in the process—Ministers, backbenchers, civil servants, interest groups and the Monopolies Commission—were all aware of a degree of 'public concern' (to use the Commission's term). As has been suggested this influence was of a generalized nature and did not really extend to the specific content of the legislation. This is particularly important when it is remembered that the Bill was designed to protect the public interest, without anyone really knowing what that was. This seems to be a crucial point emerging from this study. A number of commentators have since thrown doubt on whether the 1956 Act has been an effective piece of legislation, and even as early as 1957, the Society of Motor Manufacturers and Traders was claiming that the power of a High Court injunction to restrain price-cutters was likely to be far more effective than the old stop lists that were made illegal by the Act. (R.P.M. has of course since been virtually abolished by the 1964 Act.) A number of restrictive agreements have also managed to secure the blessing of the Court since 1956, and the Conservative government's White Paper in 1964 (Cmd. 2294) conceded that methods of circumventing the Act had been devised. (Such agreements are included in the present government's proposed legislation.) D. P. O'Brien and D. Swan, in their analysis of the effects of information agreements, have proposed various reforms which should 'help to provide the stimulus to competition which the 1956 Act has so clearly failed to do' (O'Brien, Manchester School, Sept. 1966, 306). A further criticism is that the Court now

104

proceeds at about the same rate as did the Commission prior to the 1956 Act.

It should not however be concluded that the 1956 Act has been a complete failure. Yamey and Stevens argue that it can be regarded as *politically* successful, because the government has avoided the responsibility for implementing the Monopolies Commission's recommendations, together with the 'attendant pressures from the industry concerned' (Yamey and Stevens, 1965, 141). They suggest that the businessman is also happy because he does not have to face his 'avowed enemy', the administrative process. They concede that economically the Act has also had its successes. Firstly it has encouraged the voluntary abandonment of a number of restrictive agreements (just as Mr. Heath's 1964 R.P.M. Act encouraged the tobacco manufacturers to abandon R.P.M. on cigarettes in September 1968). Secondly, decisions of the Court have resulted in increased competition in certain industries which have appeared before it, although the 'apparently limited effect' of these developments can be attributed to the skill of the legal profession in producing schemes, and to the buoyant state of the economy (Yamey and Stevens, 1965, 142). It is important to note too, that even the present Labour government has found itself in a dilemma over restrictive practices and monopolies. On the one hand it still believes in increased competition within British industry, and has therefore introduced its Restrictive Practices Bill to close certain loopholes. On the other hand it has recognized that certain so-called restrictive agreements may operate in the national interest, and it has therefore made provision in the new legislation for the Board of Trade to exempt from registration, agreements which they consider necessary to promote the carrying out of a scheme of substantial importance to the national economy. The reason why the government has been forced into this dilemma is that the threat of investigation by the Restrictive Practices Court has apparently inhibited organizations like the Little Neddies, and the Prices and Incomes Board, from proposing trading practices designed to increase efficiency. An excellent example of this dilemma is provided by the Ministry of Technology's efforts to persuade the chemical industry to exchange information about investment decisions, so that wasteful duplication can be avoided (*The Times Business News*, 15 February 1968). Yet at the same time, the government is trying to bring information agreements within the scope of the Court! In the same way, the government's policy on mergers raises problems of conflicting aims. On the one hand the government is encouraging mergers and rationalization schemes through the activity of the Industrial Reorganization Corporation, yet it has introduced monopolies legislation with the implicit aims of preventing these. The present position is that we have a proliferation of bodies with conflicting aims, with the result that according to a *Times Business News* sample of opinion (September 1968), members of the Monopolies Commission are afraid that their work is being undermined by other agencies such as the Industrial Reorganization Corporation, and the Prices and Incomes Board, as well as by *prima facie* decisions, taken in a hurry, by the Board of Trade mergers division.

The limited effects of the 1956 legislation may in large part be attributed to the so-called detailed concessions which collectively may have neutralized the principle aims of the Bill. Thus, although the Lobby rarely succeeds in getting the government to withdraw a Bill, it may have almost the same effect by way of skilful, detailed amendments. It is of course possible to put forward a convincing argument to show that this is not entirely a bad thing, as the interest groups probably have more technical knowledge than the government anyway. The evidence in this case strongly supports the view that there is a third chamber of government outside Parliament where the effective decisions are taken, although one must add the qualification that it would be wrong to ignore the role played by backbenchers.

W. J. M. Mackenzie has said that if great problems are to be tackled, then governments must be prepared to govern (*British Journal of Sociology*, vi, No. 2, [1957], 146). The evidence suggests that neither major party is willing to do this when faced with politically controversial problems. With reference to the problem of restrictive practices, Yamey and Stevens question whether it is desirable for the government to hand a problem over to the judges if it is politically controversial. The Labour government has in a similar way created extra-governmental agencies (though not of a strictly judicial nature) to deal with such politically controversial problems as a prices and incomes policy. This particular case study reveals policy making as a process of conflict and compromise, which in practice makes effective action difficult. Such action is likely to prove more difficult if governments insist on handing over what are essentially *political* problems to extra-governmental and extra-parliamentary bodies, in order to achieve a high degree of consensus between conflicting forces.

Suggestions for further reading

There are few studies solely concerned with the policy-making process though most books on British government deal with the main issues involved. Worthy of special mention are the following:

Pressure groups

FINER, S. E., (Second Edition, 1966), *Anonymous Empire*, Pall Mall Press.

This is by far the most lively and stimulating work on British pressure groups and covers the relationship between the Lobby, Whitehall, Westminster and the public.

WILSON, H. H., (1961), *Pressure Groups—The Campaign for Commercial Television*, Secker and Warburg.

A case study of the lobby which campaigned for the introduction of commercial television in Britain. It deals with the relationship between the Conservative Party and the commercial interests backing commercial television.

ECKSTEIN, H., (1960), *Pressure Group Politics. The Case of the B.M.A.*, Allen and Unwin.

This contains an interesting theoretical introduction to the study of pressure groups, as well as being a well-documented study of the role of the B.M.A. in the formation of medical policy in Britain.

Policy making

HINDELL, K., 'The Genesis of the Race Relations Bill', *Political Quarterly*, Oct./Dec. 1965, 390-405.

An analysis of the origins, stages of evolution and process of enactment of the Race Relations Bill.

VITAL, D., (1968), *The Making of British Foreign Policy*, Allen and Unwin.

An analysis of the essentially pragmatic approach to policy making in this field.

DEAKIN, N., 'The Politics of the Commonwealth Immigrants Bill', *Political Quarterly*, xxxix, No. 1, 1968, 25-45.

Deals with the opinions and events surrounding the issue of restriction of immigration into Britain.

CHAPMAN, R., 'The Bank Rate Decision of 19th September, 1957', *Public Administration*, Summer 1965.

A case study of decision making which is designed to illustrate the importance of informal discussions in the decision-making process.

Symposium sponsored by the Royal Institute of Public Administration, 'Who are the Policy Makers?', *Public Administration*, xliii, 1965.

Includes interesting contributions by Sir Edward Boyle, Sir Edward Playfair and Nevil Johnson.

CUNNINGHAM, SIR CHARLES, 'Policy and Practice', *Public Administration*, Autumn 1963.

The random reflections of a senior civil servant, on the way that policy is formulated and executed.

WALKLAND, S. A., (1968), *The Legislative Process*, Allen and Unwin.

Analyses the major elements in the legislative process.

General

SHONFIELD, A., (1965), *Modern Capitalism—The Changing Balance of Public and Private Power*, R.I.I.A. and Oxford University Press.

SHANKS, M., (1967), *The Innovators*, Penguin.

Both deserve special mention as well-argued and well-documented contributions to the discussion of problems which are central to the economic and political systems in Britain.

BUTT, R., (1967), *The Power of Parliament*, Constable.

This is an invaluable analysis of the role played by Parliament in the political system and in addition contains an excellent account of the passage of the 1964 R.P.M. Bill.

Monopoly and restrictive practices

Students seeking further information on monopolies and restrictive practices should consult:

YAMEY, B. S., and STEVENS, R. B., (1965), *The Restrictive Practices Court*, Weidenfeld and Nicolson.

An excellent study of the relationship between the judicial process and economic policy.

Also:

HUNTER, A., (1966), *Competition and the Law*, Allen and Unwin.

ROWLEY, C. K., (1966), *The British Monopolies Commission*, Allen and Unwin.

GUÉNAULT, P. H., and JACKSON, J. M., (1960), *The Control of Monopoly in the United Kingdom*, Longmans.
A comprehensive bibliography on restrictive practices can be found in :
HUTTON, G., (1966), *Source-Book on Restrictive Practices in Britain*, I.E.A. Research Monographs.

Bibliography

Books

BAILEY, S. K., (1950), *Congress Makes a Law*, New York: Columbia University Press.

BRITTAN, S., (1964), *The Treasury Under the Tories*, Penguin.

BROCK, C., (1966), *The Control of Restrictive Practices From 1956*, McGraw-Hill.

BUTT, R., (1967), *The Power of Parliament*, Constable.

CHAMBERLIN, E. H., (ed.), (1954), *Monopoly and Competition and their Regulation*, Macmillan.

EPSTEIN, L. D., (1964), *British Politics in the Suez Crisis*, Pall Mall Press.

FINER, S. E., (1966), *Anonymous Empire*, Pall Mall Press.

GINSBERG, M., (1959), *Law and Opinion in England in the 20th Century*, Stevens & Sons.

GROVE, J. W., (1962), *Government and Industry in Great Britain*, Longmans.

JOHNSON, D. MC. I., (1958), *A Doctor in Parliament*, Christopher Johnson.

KILMUIR, EARL OF, (1964), *Political Adventure*, Weidenfeld an'd Nicolson.

MACKENZIE, W. J. M. and GROVE, J. W., (1957), *Central Administration in Britain*, Longmans.

P.E.P., (1957), *Industrial Trade Associations*, P.E.P. and Allen and Unwin.

POTTER, A., (1961), *Organized Groups in British National Politics*, Faber and Faber.

ROBERTSON, D. H., (1956), *Economic Commentaries*, Staples Press.

ROSE, R., (1965), *Politics in England*, Faber and Faber.

SELF, P. and STORING, H., (1962), *The State and the Farmer*, Allen and Unwin.

SHANKS, M., (1967), *The Innovators*, Penguin.

SHONFIELD, A., (1965), *Modern Capitalism*, R.I.I.A. and Oxford University Press.

STEWART, J. D., (1958), *British Pressure Groups*, Oxford University Press.

TRUMAN, D., (1951), *The Governmental Process*, New York: Alfred A. Knopf.

WHEARE, K. C., (1955), *Government by Committee*, Oxford University Press.

YAMEY, B. S. and STEVENS, R. B., (1965), *The Restrictive Practices Court*, Weidenfeld and Nicolson.

Articles

Conservative Political Centre, 'Change is our Ally', (1954).

EASTON, D., 'An Approach to the Analysis of Political Systems', *World Politics*, ix, No. 2, (1957), 384-400.

FINER, S. E., 'The Federation of British Industries', *Political Studies*, iv, No. 1, (1965), 61-84.

MACROSTY, H. W., 'The Trust Movement in British Industry', *Fabian Pamphlet Series II*, (1907).

MACKENZIE, R. T., 'Parties, Pressure Groups and the British

Political Process', *Political Quarterly*, xxix, No. 1, (1958), 5-16.

MACKENZIE, W. J. M., 'Pressure Groups in British Government', *British Journal of Sociology*, vi, No. 2, (1955), 133-148.

O'BRIEN, D. P. and SWANN, D., 'Information Agreements— a Problem in Search of a Policy', *Manchester School*, (Sept. 1966), 285-306.

TIVEY, L. and WOHLGEMUTH, E., 'Trade Associations and Interest Groups', *Political Quarterly*, xxix, No. 1, (1958), 59-71.

Documents

Final Report of the Committee on Industry and Trade, (The Balfour Committee), Cmd. 3282.

Report of the Committee on Restraint of Trade, (The Greene Committee), (1930).

White Paper on Full Employment Policy after the War, Cmd. 6427, (1944).

Report of the Committee on Resale Price Maintenance, Cmd. 7695, (Lloyd Jacob Committee), (1949).

White Paper on Resale Price Maintenance, Cmd. 8274, (1951).

Monopolies and Restrictive Practices Commission, Report on Collective Discrimination, Cmd. 9504, (June 1955).

Second Report of the Select Committee on Estimates, (1959/60).

White Paper on Monopolies, Mergers and Restrictive Practices, Cmd. 2299, (1964).

Legal Cases

Mogul Steamship Co. v. McGregor Gow & Co., (1892), A.C. 25.

Attorney-General of the Commonwealth of Australia v. Adelaide Steamship Co. Ltd., (1913), A.C. 78.

N.W. Salt Co. Ltd. v. Electrolytic Alkali Co. Ltd., (1914), A.C. 461.

Thorne v. Motor Trade Association, (1937), A.C. 797.

9781032812373